CW01471809

GOSPEL AND CHURCH

Gospel and Church

**An evangelical evaluation of ecumenical
documents on church unity**

Hywel R. Jones

EVANGELICAL PRESS OF WALES

© Evangelical Press of Wales, 1989
First published 1989
ISBN 1 85049 064 3

Published by the Evangelical Press of Wales
Bryntirion, Bridgend, Mid Glamorgan CF31 4DX, Wales
Printed by Billing & Sons Ltd, Worcester

Contents

'What happens when a corporate body lacking a clear external standard of truth and judgement grows in strength? . . . The corporate body strives to become a standard to itself, a law to itself. In a word, it presses forward to the status of a Leviathan, that "mortal god" which Hobbes described so accurately . . . In sum: unless an infallible, inerrant Word stands above the church, judging it and proclaiming grace to it, magisterial authority is the greatest liability the church can have, for it will inevitably become the unprincipled tool and demonic reflection of sinful man.'

J. Warwick Montgomery
Ecumenicity, Evangelicals and Rome

Introduction

I am delighted to write a few words to introduce and commend this book which you hold in your hands. Centuries ago a wise man declared: 'The pen is mightier than the sword.' The events which bridge the long years from then until now have proved both the wisdom and the truth of his words. History — and church history in particular — demonstrates that when the pen is servant to a clear mind and a believing heart, and when it is wielded with integrity, clarity and sincerity, it is one of the best friends that truth (and those who seek after it) can have.

It was in the interests of truth that the author took up his pen to write this book. Indeed, he did so as one who loves the truth and has spent his life serving, promoting, and defending it. This work is no overnight venture. On the contrary, it is a mature, lucid discussion of Christian verities and their application to present-day perplexities. The author deals with these matters not only in an effective and helpful manner, but also with an unobtrusive, scholarly ability, in which penetrating insight and fidelity to Scripture are very happily combined. I have for long known and admired the writer as a fine expositor and a powerful preacher of the evangel. As the opportunity arose, I have also sat under his ministry with great profit. Furthermore, I have benefited from his writing, as he has engaged in articulate theological discussion over the years with those most in need of evangelical perspectives.

As you begin to read, you will discover that the book has come into being because my friend, the Rev. Principal Hywel Jones, is deeply concerned about the erosion of the Christian gospel by attack, not from without, but from *within* the professing Christian church. That gospel is, of course, rooted in a special revelation from God, which has been recorded for us in the Bible. It is from the Bible that we learn the great truths and facts of the gospel — the 'good news' of God's saving grace and all that He has accomplished for the redemption of His people through His Son, the Lord Jesus Christ. That makes the Bible — and our beliefs about it — very important.

In the course of this twentieth century two things have brought both the Bible and the church increasingly into the focus of attention. One is the *radical criticism* to which the Bible has been subjected by unbelieving scholarship, and the subsequent pronouncements of many churchmen in questioning the Bible's authority or denying its leading doctrines. The other factor is the *Ecumenical Movement*, which has been bending its energies to unify the denominations of the world. One serious question in the minds of many Christians concerns the place of truth — or, more precisely, the Bible — in these vast ecumenical processes. *That* is the question which this book probes and answers. From statements contained in its own official documents, the place of the Bible in the Ecumenical Movement in the twentieth century is subjected to a searching scrutiny. It does not come out of it well. In their attempts to address the dilemmas of this age, the proponents of the ecumenical message have forfeited the timeless biblical heritage of the church of God.

With extensive experience in the pastoral ministry, Hywel Jones knows that the church is a fellowship of people whose lives have been transformed by Christ, but who nevertheless need to be built up in the faith. He knows that the way God does this is through the preaching of the Word. That qualifies him to write on this subject. He has also had years of experience in preparing men for the ministry of the Word and in teaching theology in a wide variety of academic situations. This further qualifies him to probe into the momentous questions which he handles in this book. In addition, his work has meant that he has lived for some years in Scotland and Wales as well as London. His contact with the church in the United Kingdom is therefore broadly based.

These factors combine to make this an important and valuable work. It is important because it draws our attention to questions and alerts us to dangers with which every single evangelical Christian in the Western world must become familiar. We *must* become aware of them if we are to retain the only gospel of salvation and the church which that gospel (when accompanied with God's power and blessing) brings into being in this sad world.

But the importance and value of this work is vastly enhanced by the simple yet alarming fact that, to the best of my knowledge, no other book of this type has been produced by the evangelical world. This is the only serious, scholarly, and carefully researched work which we have to help us evaluate the issues it confronts. It is the only book available to us, conducted from a theological and historical viewpoint and from within a truly biblical framework, which provides a treatment of the most serious Christian issue of the day. It breaks new ground. It is my earnest prayer that it will bring forth a rich, rewarding harvest and help promote a return to that biblical faith which alone will produce a biblical church.

J. DOUGLAS MACMILLAN
Free Church College, Edinburgh
December 1988

Preface

Underlying this book is the conviction that current ecumenical thinking about the church is in conflict with what the Bible teaches about the gospel. In the pages that follow various inter-church documents are examined in order to present the evidence in support of such a serious charge. The title of this book — *Gospel and Church* — not only points to the primacy of the gospel and its supremacy over the church, but also to the harmony which ought to exist between them. The gospel creates the church and is to be expressed *by* the church *to* the world.

I have many people to thank for their help in connection with this book. First and foremost, I want to acknowledge the encouragement of the late Rev. Dr Martyn Lloyd-Jones, who urged me to consider the subject treated in the first chapter of this book and in many ways influenced my thinking on the other issues as well. I hope that his widow, Mrs Bethan Lloyd-Jones, will find pleasure in seeing it in print in this her ninetieth year.

I am also conscious of the help of my faculty colleagues at the London Theological Seminary, with whom parts of this material have been discussed from time to time. I especially want to thank Rev. G.S. Harrison, M.A. B.Litt., for reading the manuscript and making a number of helpful comments on it.

I am indebted to the Evangelical Press of Wales for their willingness to publish this book, and to the editorial and office staff there for their help. The Evangelical Movement of Wales and the British Evangelical Council have provided further stimulation for this work. I trust that this book will further their witness — both separately and together.

Dr Nigel Cameron has given me permission to incorporate in a revised and expanded form an article which appeared in *Evangel*.

Mrs Marilyn Park of Maryland, USA, produced a most presentable typescript from an untidy manuscript and I am most grateful to her.

Rev. Douglas Macmillan, Professor at the Free Church College, Edinburgh, has written an introduction which exceeds whatever friendship may expect of him.

My father, William Jones (who died in January 1987), would have wholeheartedly endorsed the aim of this book. In completing it, I have been particularly aware that I have, as it were, been speaking for him.

But finally, I want to dedicate this book to Nansi, who has stood with me for these gospel principles for over twenty-five years of our life together.

HYWEL R. JONES
London Theological Seminary
April 1989

1
Scripture and Tradition

1963 was an important year in ecumenical discussion of the nature and status of the Bible. In July of that year, the Fourth World Conference on Faith and Order, one of a series of conferences organized by the World Council of Churches (WCC), was held at Montreal in Canada. One of the subjects studied there was 'Scripture, Tradition and Traditions'.[1]

This was not the first occasion for an ecumenical gathering to consider the Bible. Prior to Montreal, a number of conferences had been held in the years immediately following the Second World War, and the work put in to these culminated in a conference which was held at Wadham College, Oxford, in 1949. A statement was issued by this meeting entitled 'Guiding Principles for the Interpretation of the Bible'.[2] It was the fruit of discussions about how to approach certain social and political questions. It was fairly brief and general in character. No Roman Catholics contributed to it, though the Orthodox Churches were represented. Following Montreal, a number of study groups and plenary Faith and Order Conferences met to do further work on aspects of the statement which it had produced. These were held at Bristol (U.K.) in 1967, at Louvain (Belgium) in 1971 and at Bangalore (India) in 1978. They concentrated on hermeneutics, authority and the relation between the Old and New Testaments respectively.

Though it was one conference among others, Montreal was a watershed for ecumenical study of the Bible in two major respects. On the one hand, a *breakthrough* was effected there and, on the other hand, a decisive *breach*. We shall consider each of these in turn.

13

THE BREAKTHROUGH

All the churches of the WCC are doctrinally related to the Bible in one way or another. In view of this, an approach to the Scriptures which is common to all participants in the ecumenical venture is essential. The Bible is therefore a vital matter not only for evangelicalism, but also for ecumenism — though not in the same way, as we shall see. Lukas Vischer writes: 'To form a relationship of effective common witness, it is essential that the churches reach a common understanding of the authority and use of the Bible in the life and witness of the Church.' [3]

Two things, which happened at Montreal, helped to bring about the breakthrough which we are seeking to describe. *First*, there were Roman Catholics present. While they had only taken up observer status (unlike the Orthodox who were full members of the Council), they could not have been more active. As a result, it was possible for the first time to perceive the ecumenical problem in all its aspects. *Secondly*, the Montreal conference gave its attention to one of the issues which had created the basic divide in the Reformation between the Roman Catholics (and therefore also the Orthodox) on the one hand and the Protestants on the other. This was the relationship between Scripture and Tradition. Did God reveal Himself and His will sufficiently and supremely in Holy Scripture alone, or by the traditions of the apostles handed down orally in the church as well (see pp.27, 32ff.; cf. also pp.23ff.)? If this deadlock could be lifted, then progress could be achieved not only on the Scripture-Tradition issue, but on every other theological issue as well.

Given a subject with such a degree of controversy attached to it, one might think that with only the Wadham statement behind it, the delegates were taking an exceedingly bold step. However, this was not the case. Much had happened between 1949 and 1962/3 with regard to the Scripture-Tradition question on both sides of the Reformation divide, and so the risk involved in tackling the subject head-on was minimal. Apart from the effect generated by the ecumenical phenomenon and experience, two events need to be noted in this change.

The first event was the Third World Faith and Order Conference which was held in 1952 at Lund in Sweden. This demonstrated what had been happening in *Protestantism* with

14

regard to our subject. Secondly, there was another gathering — a council, not a conference — namely, the unexpected and famed Second Vatican Council which met in the autumn of 1962. This gave an indication of what was happening in *Roman Catholicism* on the same matter. Though barely six months elapsed between the Council and the Montreal conference, theologians were well aware of each other's views prior to these gatherings. A new route was opened up to study the relationship between Scripture and Tradition. Indeed, this was evidently the case with Vatican II.

The Lund conference, with 'Schism, Heresy and Apostasy' as its subject, gave to many an experience of a theological impasse, because the representatives of each church viewed these matters from the perspective of their own denominational history. This was described in a British journal of the time under the caption 'The Ecumenical Dead-End Kids'.[4] As a result, a resolution was passed to set up a theological commission with the task of exploring more deeply 'the resources for further ecumenical discussion to be found in that common history which we have as Christians'.[5]

When this approved motion reached the Working Committee in 1953, it was decided to appoint an interim committee 'to study the problem of tradition in all its biblical and historical aspects, paying particular attention to the problem as it has been put before us in recent literature in order to bring out the importance and need of such a study for ecumenical understanding.'[6] This committee was set up in two sections, one in North America and the other in Europe. They approached this theme in differing, but complementary ways. The American group viewed the subject from a historical standpoint; the Europeans treated it theologically. Their reports came before the Montreal conference.

Clearly, enough had been said and done to encourage Montreal to tackle the subject of Scripture and Tradition from a standpoint other than that of *sola Scriptura*, i.e. Scripture versus Tradition. Coupled with this, of course, was the awareness of what had happened at the opening session of the Second Vatican Council where it seemed that Scripture was being spoken of favourably *vis-à-vis* Tradition. The Montreal report could state: 'We are . . . aware that in Roman Catholic theology the concept of tradition is undergoing serious reconsideration.' [7]

Prior to Montreal, Father Yves M. Congar, the author of a massive work entitled *Tradition and Traditions*[8] had submitted a comment on the reports of the two working groups which were to be tabled at the conference. In that comment he had referred to the writings of G.H. Tavard (who was at Montreal) and Karl Rahner on the subject of Tradition. These progressive Roman Catholic theologians were very influential in the run-up to Vatican II and afterwards.

We must now give a brief summary of what happened at the opening session of Vatican II. Of the sixteen documents[9] which emerged from the Council, only two are dignified with the title 'Dogmatic Constitution'. These are entitled *Lumen Gentium* (The Light of the Nations) and *Dei Verbum* (The Word of God). They relate to the Church and to revelation respectively. They are most important promulgations and the distinctive theology of Vatican II is to be found in them.

Relatively speaking, neither document is very long in terms of number of words, yet they took more time to reach their final form than any of the rest.

Dei Verbum (with which we are concerned) is five times shorter than *Lumen Gentium*, and yet it took one more year for it to be finalized. This was not due to the fact that it had not been discussed during the second session of the Council, but rather because the statement that was initially tabled on the Scripture-Tradition issue had run into such difficulty that the whole subject had to be reinvestigated.

This prepared statement, entitled *De Fontibus Revelationis* (Concerning the Sources of Revelation) was bitterly opposed when it came before the Council. Cardinal Liénart expressed his opposition in the following words:

> This schema [i.e. the prepared document] does not please me. It is not adequate to the matter it purports to deal with, namely, Scripture and Tradition. There are not and never have been two sources of revelation. The Word of God is the unique source of revelation. This schema is a cold and scholastic formula, while revelation is a supreme gift of God — God speaking directly to us. We should be thinking more along the lines of our separated brothers who have such a love and veneration for the Word of God. Our duty now is to cultivate the faith of our people and cease to condemn.[10]

This protest and approach to the question of Scripture-Tradition was so strongly supported in the Council that it became necessary for the Pope to intervene. He decided to withdraw the offending schema and appointed a special commission to revise it. Progressive theologians were appointed to this working group and the result was *Dei Verbum*. With this and Lund behind it, the Montreal conference could take up the Scripture-Tradition question without fear of being stabbed in the back.

Commenting on both *Dei Verbum* and the Montreal statement, Flesseman-van Leer writes:

> Both statements deal with identical or similar problems; both are official statements and can therefore be considered as giving a general overall picture of the respective positions. One cannot expect bold and new theological insights in documents of this kind, but exactly for that reason they are a gauge for present-day thinking.[11]

DEI VERBUM

Dei Verbum consists of a short preface and twenty-six articles arranged in six chapters. These concern:

- revelation (chapter 1)
- its transmission (chapter 2)
- Scripture — its inspiration and interpretation (chapters 3—5)
- Scripture in the life of the church (chapter 6)

What we must try to do is to examine this statement to see if it represents a real shift from the position promulgated at the Council of Trent in 1546[12] and, if so, whether this is a move towards the theology of the Reformation on the Scripture-Tradition question. We must look at what it says about revelation, Tradition and Scripture.

Before we do this, there is one detailed but important matter which we must examine. It is well known that *Dei Verbum* encouraged personal and private reading of the Scriptures by the faithful, and the setting up of societies for their translation and distribution — even jointly with 'separated brethren' (i.e. those who are not Roman Catholics). This has come to be regarded as positive proof not only of a real change in Rome, but also of a move in a Protestant direction, so to speak. What needs to be borne in mind on this point, however, is that it is *still* the magisterium of the Roman Catholic Church which alone has the grace and right to interpret those Scriptures authentically. This is classic Roman Catholicism and is referred to in the very chapter of *Dei Verbum* (chapter 6) where such reading and translation of the Scriptures are encouraged. Article 25 declares:

> It devolves on sacred bishops, 'who have the apostolic teaching', to give the faithful entrusted to them suitable instruction in the right use of the divine books, especially the New Testament and above all the Gospels, through translations of the sacred texts. Such versions are to be provided with necessary and fully adequate explanations . . .[13]

We must now consider what *Dei Verbum* has to say about revelation, Tradition and Scripture.

I. Revelation

Dei Verbum is the most important official statement ever issued by the Roman Catholic Church on this crucial subject, which lies not only at the centre of contemporary theological discussion, but also of Christianity itself. The first paragraph is worth quoting in full, as it contains the constitutive elements of the doctrine which is unfolded in the articles that follow it. It is:

> In His goodness and wisdom, God chose to reveal Himself and to make known to us the hidden purpose of His will . . . by which through Christ, the Word made flesh, man has access to the Father in the Holy Spirit and comes to share in the divine nature . . . Through this revelation, therefore, the invisible God . . . out of the abundance of His love speaks to men as friends . . . and lives among them . . . so that He may invite and take them into fellowship with Himself. This plan of revelation is realized by deeds and words having an inner unity: the deeds wrought by God in the history of salvation manifest and confirm the teaching and realities signified by the words, while the words proclaim the deeds and clarify the mystery contained in them. By this revelation then, the deepest truth about God and the salvation of man is made clear to us in Christ, who is the Mediator and at the same time the fullness of all revelation.[14]

The following six emphases appear in this statement:

1. Revelation is set in a Trinitarian framework. Each Person of the Trinity is seen at work either in its disclosure or in its reception. It is only the absence of any reference to the Spirit in connection with the activity of revelation that prevents us saying

'both . . . and' in the immediately preceding sentence instead of 'either . . . or'. However, it is only fair to say that the Spirit's work is clearly affirmed in Article 7 of *Dei Verbum*, but it is so there with regard to *both* Tradition and Scripture.

2. Revelation depends upon the sovereign act of God, and it is effected because that sovereignty is clothed with goodness, wisdom and abundant love.

3. Revelation is both based upon and focused in the Person of Christ, 'the Word made flesh', through whom all revelation comes and in whom it reaches its acme.

4. The necessity of revelation is alluded to in the description of God as 'invisible'; its progressive character is indicated by the words 'the history of salvation'; and its finality is implied in what is said about Christ being its 'fullness'.

5. The content of revelation is described in terms of 'God and His saving purpose, and this is accomplished by deeds and words in close and specified relationship to each other.'

6. The purpose of revelation is presented as the bringing of man into fellowship with and likeness to God.

Apart from the minor criticism which we have offered, and the absence of any mention of faith as the response to revelation under point 6 above (this is given separate treatment in Article 5), all these statements are quite unexceptionable as a summary of revelation. To leave the matter here, however, would be incredibly naïve. Every credal or confessional statement is a *piece of history*. By this phrase we mean far more than the obvious fact that they are part of the church's history. The fact is that every such statement is *historically conditioned*. It bears the marks of the circumstances in which it was formulated, the conflicts which necessitated it, and the thinking of those who drew it up and their purpose in doing so. This holds as good for *Dei Verbum* as for the Chalcedonian Definition on the Person of Christ (AD 451). It is mainly points 5 and 6 above which are signposts to the situation in which this statement on divine revelation is set.

The statements of people actually involved in the formulation of *Dei Verbum* are a great help here. Two of these were Bishop B.C. Butler and Joseph Ratzinger. They were appointed by

Pope John's elected commission to serve on a sub-commission. We shall make use of their comments.

Bishop Butler has a chapter entitled 'Revelation and Inspiration' in his valuable book *The Theology of Vatican II*.[15] With regard to *Dei Verbum*'s treatment of revelation, he comments that it 'does not begin, as a manual of dogmatic theology might, with a scholastic definition of the meaning of "divine revelation" considered as a term of general connotation'.[16]

Butler is here referring to the theology which lay behind Liénart's protest and the progressives' thinking in the Council which was expressed in the preface to *Dei Verbum*. The emphasis in the preface is unambiguously placed on the interpersonal character of revelation — what Butler, echoing (but significantly reversing) Martin Buber's terminology, calls the 'Thou-and-I-relationship'.

Ratzinger makes exactly the same point in his commentary on this chapter in *Commentary on the Documents of Vatican II*.[17] There he refers to the work of René Latourelle who has shown with painstaking detail the *correspondence* between Vatican I and II on this matter. (The first Vatican Council was held in 1870. It issued the decree on papal infallibility.) Ratzinger also points out that Latourelle has mentioned the *differences* between the two Councils. These differences show how thinking on the subject of revelation has undergone a change in the intervening ninety years. Two verbal changes demonstrate this. One is more minor than the other, but neither is without real significance. First, Vatican I attributes revelation to 'goodness and wisdom'; Vatican II to 'His goodness and wisdom'. This emphasizes the personal element. Secondly, Vatican I speaks of the content of revelation as 'the eternal decree of His will'; Vatican II changes this to the 'Sacrament[um] of His will'. Ratzinger's comment on this latter change is worth noting. He says: 'Instead of the legalistic view that sees revelation largely as the issuing of divine decrees, we have a sacramental view, which sees law and grace, word and deed, message and sign, the person and his utterance within the one comprehensive unity of the mystery.'[18]

A further contrast concerns the position which the knowledge of God, obtained by the exercise of man's reason, occupies in the two Councils' definitions. In Vatican I it comes at the beginning; in Vatican II at the end. One cannot escape the feeling that it has been appended rather summarily in Vatican II, and not integrated with what precedes it. But the fact that it *is* included is important. For all the emphasis on divine revelation, natural theology is not repudiated. There are still two ways to know God.

The leading characteristic, then, of this 'new' emphasis is its insistence that divine revelation is *from* a Person, *of* a person, *to* a person, and that revelation is the means by which these persons come together. It is generally believed that there was an earlier view of revelation which did not emphasize this, and indeed was prevented from appreciating it by its conviction that revelation consisted in revealed *truths* which could not be known in any other way.[19] An example of this can be seen in a passage quoted by Bishop Butler and in his own comment upon that passage. He refers to Tanquerey's scholastic definition of revelation, namely that revelation is 'the manifestation of some truth made to us by God through a supernatural illumination of our mind'.[20] He then proceeds to characterize the two views pictorially as follows: 'We are not in the schoolroom where a divine philosopher, himself unseen, dictates abstract ideas to pupils of high intelligence. We seem rather to be in the original paradise, where an infinitely loving God calls to us, accepts us as his friends, woos us to his friendship.'[21]

Bishop Butler finds evidence in *Dei Verbum* of tension between these two view of revelation. He writes: 'The first chapter of *De Divina Revelatione* shows signs of a conflict between a conceptualist and a more biblical notion of revelation.'[22]

As the ground on which this verdict is based, he refers to the latent ambiguity in the word *revelation* for it can mean 'either the act of revealing or the truths revealed'.[23] The Constitution does use it in both ways. The second sentence of the opening paragraph which we have quoted is an example of the former. For an example of the latter we may quote from Article 6:

> Through divine revelation God chose to show forth and communicate Himself and the eternal decisions of His will regarding the salvation of men. That is to say, He chose 'to share those divine treasures which totally transcend the understanding of the human mind.'[24]

The latter part of the above statement is a quotation from Vatican I. In *Dei Verbum* the weight of emphasis, however, falls on the personalist rather than the propositional element. This is also in harmony with modern Protestant theologizing about the nature of revelation.

II. Tradition

To note the full title of the second chapter of *Dei Verbum* is essential for a proper study of its contents. It is 'The Transmission of Divine Revelation'. All it contains must therefore be related to the reality of revelation as presented in the previous chapter. The second chapter aims to supply an answer to the important question: 'How can God in Christ be known today?' The opening words of this chapter declare: 'In His gracious goodness, God has seen to it that what He had revealed for the salvation of all nations would abide perpetually in its full integrity and be handed on to all generations.'[25] The question which this statement evokes is 'How does this come about?'

The answer of this chapter — and it is the classic answer of Roman Catholicism — is that it is *not only* by Scripture that this is effected, *but also* by Tradition, and so the chapter draws out the relevance of both for the process of transmission of revelation. In the course of doing this, the relationship between Tradition and Scripture is also discussed.

Because it is Tradition that is under consideration at this juncture, we will try to exclude as many references to Scripture as possible, as Scripture will be discussed later.

One sentence in this second chapter of *Dei Verbum* seems to supply a convenient framework for the treatment of the subject now before us. It is:

> Hence there exist a close connection and communication between sacred tradition and sacred Scripture. For both of them, flowing from the same divine wellspring, in a certain way merge into a unity and tend toward the same end.[26]

This sentence presents us with three elements regarding Tradition, namely, its source, unity, and purpose.

1. *The Source of Tradition (and Scripture)*

Article 7 deals with this subject.[27] It describes the source of both Tradition and Scripture as being *from* God *through* Christ and *by* the Holy Spirit. Christ the Lord is the One 'in whom the full revelation of the supreme God is brought to completion'. He also initiates the process by which that revelation is transmitted

— a revelation which He Himself was and which He proclaimed to others. He commissioned apostles 'to preach to all men that gospel which is the source of all saving truth and moral teaching', and they carried out this charge 'by their oral preaching, by example, and by ordinances'. Some of the apostles 'committed the message of salvation to writing', as did others who are termed 'apostolic men', but both groups did so 'under the inspiration of the same Holy Spirit'. This is the first stage in the process of the transmission of revelation.

It is important to note, however, that this view of Tradition is *implicitly* already larger than what Scripture would contain. The fulfilment of the Lord's commission is not linked exclusively with the inscripturation of the message of salvation. It also includes, and this before the other, the handing on by the apostles not only 'what they had received from the lips of Christ', but 'from living with Him, and from what He did, or what they had learned through the prompting of the Holy Spirit'. This is sacred Tradition — *oral* Tradition which is extra to *written* Scripture.

The second stage concerns the bishops. Though the Constitution does not say that the apostles appointed bishops as formally as they had themselves been appointed by Christ (it says they *left* them as their successors), it does claim that the apostles ' "[handed] over their own teaching role" to them'. This was done 'to keep the gospel forever whole and alive within the Church'. So we are left with a body of material, some written and some unwritten, which in its entirety can be traced backwards from the bishops, a continuing order in the church, through the apostles, to God in Christ. This puts extra-scriptural material in the same category as Scripture and, therefore, on the same basis of authority.

2. *The Unity of Tradition and Scripture*

The presence of the words 'in a certain way'[28] in the quotation which we are analyzing prevents a *total* identification between Scripture and Tradition. The inclusion of the phrase nevertheless amounts to an assertion that Scripture and Tradition coalesce. They are therefore not to be totally separated. That they do merge is made clear by the following words: 'Sacred tradition and Sacred Scripture form one sacred deposit of the word of God, which is committed to the Church.'[29] We must enquire how this comes about and we shall focus on how Tradition can be called 'the word of God', as Scripture's right to that designation may be taken for granted. The answer to this question is composed of three elements, which may be termed the original content, the development, and the use, of Tradition.

a) The Original Content of Tradition

Article 8 puts forward a case which is based on 2 Thessalonians 2:15, where Paul speaks of the traditions he had taught 'by word, or our epistle'. In the light of this text, the Article claims that what the apostles gained from Christ — in ways that were open to them alone — was of the same character, whether it was subsequently committed to writing in Scripture, *or* passed on orally. Therefore, *both* can rightly be termed 'the word of God'. Its contents are described as follows: 'Now what was handed on by the apostles includes everything which contributes to the holiness of life, and the increase in faith of the People of God.'[30]

b) The Continuing Development of Tradition

The above quotation continues: 'And so the Church, in her teaching, life and worship, perpetuates and hands on to all generations all that she herself is, all that she believes.' There is a link here between the teaching, life and worship of the church subsequent to the New Testament and the preaching, example and ordinances of the apostles as recorded in the New Testament. Now to admit that what the apostles taught orally was *more* than what they set down in Scripture is obvious and incontestable; but to assert that there is identity and harmony between that oral teaching and what the church subsequently teaches (and is!) is quite another matter. This is what is claimed in the above quotation, and it is explained in the following words: 'This tradition which comes from the apostles develops in the Church with the help of the Holy Spirit. For there is a growth in the understanding of the realities and the words which have been handed down.'[31]

The assertion here is that this growing understanding is the result of the activity of the Holy Spirit. This is a massive claim. Bishop Butler makes the point that this paragraph in Article 8 is 'practically a précis of Newman's theory of the development of doctrine'.[32] The essence of this assertion is that a developing tradition is the Word of God not only because it is in harmony

24

with apostolic teaching, but also because it is an unfolding of it. It is in this way that the dogmas of papal infallibility, and the perpetual virginity and bodily assumption of Mary are substantiated. It is this line of reasoning which makes us question the validity of this theology of Tradition.

c) The Use of Tradition

Under this heading all that needs to be done is to show that Sacred Tradition is used in much the same way as sacred Scripture. This appears in the following statements from Articles 8 and 9, each of which concerns Tradition:

> This happens [i.e. development and growth] through the contemplation and study made by believers, who treasure these things in their hearts . . ., through the intimate understanding of spiritual things they experience, and through the preaching of those who have received through episcopal succession the sure gift of truth . . . The words of the Holy Fathers witness to the living presence of this tradition, whose wealth is poured into the practice and life of the believing and praying Church . . . it is not from sacred Scripture alone that the Church draws her certainty about everything which has been revealed. Therefore both sacred tradition and sacred Scripture are to be accepted and venerated with the same sense of devotion and reverence.[33]

This means that the material studied for the discerning of dogma includes what is added to Scripture as well as Scripture itself.

3. The Purpose of Tradition and Scripture

Their goal is to perfect the Church. '[Both] are like a mirror in which the pilgrim Church on earth looks at God, from whom she has received everything, until she is brought finally to see Him as He is, face to face . . .'[34]

By them, 'as the centuries succeed one another, the Church constantly moves forward toward the fullness of divine truth until the words of God reach their complete fulfillment in her.'[35] This points in the direction of both being *necessary* for the life of the Church which must regard them both as God's self-disclosure.

*　　*　　*　　*　　*　　*

We are now in a position to consider the view of Tradition as put forward in this document.

25

The use of the word 'Tradition' in the singular and in its capitalized form represents a decided shift from the position of Trent and Vatican I on this subject. It may be compared to what we have noted in relation to revelation. There, as here, what is presented is a living reality rather than expressed propositions. In this way, *tradita* (things handed down) can be likened to *revelata* (things revealed), and *traditio* (tradition) to *revelatio* (revelation). Ratzinger comments on this change as follows:

> Vatican II starts from an abstract concept, whereas Trent was concerned with the concrete phenomenon, the actually existing traditions, by which it meant the form of the Church's life as it was actually practised.[36]

While the concept of Vatican II may be termed abstract, it should not be thought of as theoretical. It is a rather dynamic concept. It is a Spirit-superintended process which links the present with the past on one hand, and, as it has not yet reached its climax, with the future on the other. Such a concept diverts attention from the particular traditions themselves. It also makes it easier to believe in their continuity with the past, even though this cannot be demonstrated from the historical or literary point of view. Tradition is an all-embracing concept, a developing and enveloping, unfolding and enfolding reality. This is reflected in the way in which Tradition is always placed before Scripture in this chapter of *Dei Verbum*. Indeed, it is said that by Tradition 'the Church's full canon of the sacred books is known, and the sacred writings themselves are more profoundly understood and *unceasingly* made active in her' (italics mine).[37] Tradition is the dominant idea in the transmission of revelation, and Scripture is but a part of it. This is reinforced by the claim in Article 12 that in interpreting Scripture, account must be taken of 'the living tradition of the whole Church.'[38] Bishop Butler expresses this point as follows:

> In fact, then, Sacred Tradition should not be distinguished from Scripture as though they were two distinct realities, but only as a whole is distinguishable from one of its constituents. The relevant theological question is not: 'What does tradition give us that Scripture does not contain?', but 'What is the function of Scripture within the total fact of tradition?'[39]

In his book *Holy Writ or Holy Church*,[40] Father G.H. Tavard maintains that this was the Church's view on this subject prior to the fourteenth century. However, it may be noted that this position affords no protection against the Protestant charge that the traditions which have resulted from the process of transmission have distorted the original deposit of apostolic teaching, whether these found expression in Scripture or not. Ratzinger admits this, and instances the opposition of Oscar Cullmann and J.K.S. Reid. The poignancy of the situation becomes particularly evident in the face of the following claim made for the magisterium:

> The task of authentically interpreting the Word of God, whether written or handed on, has been entrusted exclusively to the living teaching office of the Church, whose authority is exercised in the name of Jesus Christ.[41]

From Tradition and Scripture as God's revelation, we are brought to the Church as its embodiment and interpreter.

III. Scripture

In chapters 3-5 of *Dei Verbum* the Bible itself is the focus of attention. The fourth and fifth chapters are concerned with the Old and New Testaments respectively, and the divine origin and inspiration of each is declared. We shall concentrate on the third chapter, which is entitled 'The Divine Inspiration and Interpretation of Sacred Scripture'. It is to that statement that Bishop Butler's question as to whether the Catholic Church is committed to a kind of biblical fundamentalism is related.[42]

The Roman Catholic Church has always upheld the full infallibility of Holy Scripture. Neither of the two great divisions within Christendom occurred over this doctrine. It was held by the Council of Trent, and by Vatican I which declared that the Scriptures were to be regarded as sacred by the Church 'not because, having been carefully composed by mere human industry, they were afterwards approved by her authority, nor merely because they contain revelation, with no admixture of error, but because, having been written by the inspiration of the Holy Ghost, they have God for their author.'[43] This is endorsed in the *New Catholic Encyclopaedia* of 1967 in the following words:

> The inerrancy of Scripture has been the constant teaching of the Fathers, the theologians, and recent popes in their encyclicals on Biblical studies (Leo XIII, *Providentissimus Deus*; Benedict XV, *Spiritus Paracletus* and Pius XII, *Divino Afflante Spiritu*).[44]

Vatican II is not wanting in this respect either. Article 11 of *Dei Verbum* declares that 'the books of both the Old and New Testaments in their entirety, with all their parts' were 'written under the inspiration of the Holy Spirit', and therefore 'have God for their author . . . it follows that the books of Scripture must be acknowledged as teaching firmly, faithfully, and without error that truth which God wanted put into the sacred writings for the sake of our salvation.'[45]

In spite of these unambiguous affirmations, there is real point in Bishop Butler's comment, for Leo XIII was Pope at the time of the rise and flourishing of what is referred to as 'the modernist movement in the Roman Catholic Church', and his encyclical *Providentissimus Deus* appeared in the very same year in which Alfred Loisy had been deprived of his professorship in the *Institut Catholique*. Pius X, Leo XIII's successor, pursued an even more rigorous policy. He appointed conservative theologians to Leo's Biblical Commission, condemned Father George Tyrrell, banned even a moderate use of biblical criticism in his decree *Lamentabili*, and denounced the whole system as heretical in his encyclical *Pascendi Gregis*. His strictures were carried into effect through councils of vigilance in every diocese, and the imposition of an anti-modernist oath on all clerics in 1910. Thus the movement was practically extinguished.[46]

However, this crisis was never really resolved, and even in 1961 professors at the Biblical Institute in Rome were banned. Pius XII's decree, generally referred to as the Magna Carta of Catholic biblical scholarship, maintains the traditional position of the magisterium while allowing greater freedom to biblical scholars. The same kind of tension is found in *Dei Verbum*. On the one hand, the inspiration of Scripture is endorsed, but on the other, the humanness of the Scriptures is recognized, and the consequent need for the interpreter to 'investigate what meaning the sacred writer intended to express and actually expressed in particular circumstances as he used contemporary literary forms in accordance with the situation of his own time and culture.'[47] This amounts to a limitation of inerrancy. 'The books of Scripture' teach 'without error that truth which God wanted put into the sacred writings for the sake of our salvation' — but no more. Only what is necessary to salvation is set down inerrantly in Scripture. This loophole enables the Roman Catholic biblical scholar to operate in areas which were previously forbidden and to work in conjunction with Protestant biblical scholars — but always within the limits of Roman Catholic dogma, as the case of Hans Küng makes clear. Article 19 of *Dei Verbum* endorses the view which sees the Gospels as documents composed in the light of the post-Easter faith of the church, but maintains that their contents are 'true and sincere'. According to B.C. Butler, *Dei Verbum* exhibits an attempt 'to steer a course between the Scylla of radicalism and the Charybdis of Fundamentalism.'[48]

Dei Verbum is a statement which does strike out into a new world and in a new spirit. But it does this while retaining its links with classical Roman Catholic dogma as expressed in Trent and Vatican I. The change visible in Vatican II is not superficial, but neither is it substantial. Flesseman-van Leer has summed up the position nicely. She writes:

> The assertion of the constitution that only the Magisterium can authentically interpret the Tradition implies that, in the final resort, the Tradition is identical with the teaching of the Magisterium.

Later on she writes:

> As long as that possibility [i.e. that Tradition includes truths not in Scripture] has to be kept open, the Tridentine concept of Tradition and its quantitative thinking is not really overcome; no more is it possible to bind Tradition in a strict way to Scripture, let alone allow it to stand under its judgment. Consequently, the assertion that the ultimate source of faith is the Word of God, deposited in the togetherness of Tradition and Scripture does not sound convincing, for ultimately Scripture is dispensable.[49]

For all that *Dei Verbum* says about Scripture, it is not given supremacy over the Church. The Church/magisterium is still supreme. The Reformation conflict is still valid.

We turn now to the Montreal statement to see how Scripture and Tradition are dealt with there.

THE MONTREAL STATEMENT[50]

The Montreal statement on 'Scripture, Tradition and Traditions' is the second of five section reports presented to WCC member churches for their study. The statement is set out in 39 paragraphs, numbered 38-76, and consists of an introduction, three main sections and an appendix. Because of lack of con-

ference time, only the first of its main sections was fully discussed and supported. The other two were generally recommended
for study.

The appendix is an appeal to member churches to examine the
content of their own Christian education programmes to see
whether they truly reflect an ecumenical vision and concern. The
introduction identifies the theme of the statement as 'the problem of the one Tradition and the many traditions'.[51] It also provides a kind of glossary for the three variants of the word 'tradition' used in the report. We shall refer to this later. The three
main sections are entitled 'Scripture, Tradition and Traditions',
'The Unity of Tradition and the Diversity of Traditions' and
'The Christian Tradition and Cultural Diversity'. This third section is an important statement with regard to the missionary task
of the church, but as our concern is with the linking of Scripture
with Tradition, we shall pass by it for the time being and concentrate on the other two sections. In these, Tradition is given the
lion's share of attention. However, we shall begin with what is
said about Scripture.

In terms of length, the treatment of Scripture consists only of
the seven sentences which comprise paragraph 42. It is here
reproduced almost in full:

> God has revealed himself in the history of the people of God in
> the Old Testament and in Christ Jesus, his Son, the mediator bet-
> ween God and man. God's mercy and God's glory are the begin-
> ning and end of our own history. The testimony of prophets and
> apostles inaugurated the Tradition of his revelation. The once-
> for-all disclosure of God in Jesus Christ inspired the apostles and
> disciples to give witness to the revelation given in the person and
> work of Christ. No one could, and no one can, 'say that Jesus is
> Lord, save by the Holy Spirit' (1 Cor. 12:3). The oral and written
> tradition of the prophets and apostles under the guidance of the
> Holy Spirit led to the formation of Scriptures and to the
> canonization of the Old and New Testaments as the Bible of the
> Church. The very fact that Tradition precedes the Scriptures
> points to the significance of tradition, but also to the Bible as the
> treasure of the Word of God.[52]

This is nowhere near as full as *Dei Verbum*. It must be borne
in mind, however, that the above statement was the work of
days and not years. Yet more could surely have been said, and it
must be remembered that the matter was thoroughly discussed.

Shortage of time, therefore, cannot totally absolve Montreal. This paragraph must face the questions it begs. But there is another explanation of the brevity of the report at this point. In her essay in *Holy Book and Holy Tradition*[53] Ellen Flesseman-van Leer mentions the fact that the main problem Montreal faced was not the nature of Scripture. Montreal, she argues, did not need to emphasize the supreme priority of Scripture. It was rather a problem of the one Tradition *vis-à-vis* the many traditions. However, she admits that the report is surprisingly tentative and attributes this fact to the effect which the presence of representatives of Orthodox Churches had upon the conference.

We shall now consider the contents of the report in relation to revelation, inspiration and authority.

1. Scripture and Revelation

Revelation is regarded (though not specified) as the necessary precursor of Scripture. In other words, if there had not been any revelation, there could not have been any Scripture. But what exactly is revelation?

i) The *essence* of revelation is that it is the self-disclosure of God. The opening sentence of paragraph 42 (see opposite) makes this clear. It refers to Israel's history and Christ's coming in such terms. The next sentence is rather isolated and vague. It speaks of God's revelation in relation to His mercy and His glory. Are these its motive and aim? The report does not make this clear. It then links these with 'the beginning and end of our own history'. That expression needs to be integrated with God's revelation to Israel and His revelation in Christ (which are mentioned in the first sentence). It also needs to be expressed in more personal rather than philosophical terms — that is to say, God reveals Himself to us in mercy in order to bring us to know Him and His glory. All that makes *Dei Verbum* throb is lacking here. However, though it could be much more 'personalist' at this point, it is not because the 'propositional' view is favoured. Paragraph 67 states: 'The content of the Tradition cannot be exactly defined, for the reality it transmits can never be fully contained in propositional forms.'[54]

ii) The *character* of revelation is described as historical and personal in the sense that it is conveyed in the history of Israel, and in Christ. With regard to its historical aspect, though there is a welcome emphasis on the time-space reality of revelation, there is no mention of what was revelatory in that history. Was it deeds or words, or both? This is a deficiency. It is an example of the *lack of precision* which can be seen elsewhere in this statement.

With regard to revelation in Christ, there is an unambiguous insistence that it is to be found in His Person and work, and that it is of a 'once-for-all' nature.[55] While this must include the element of *finality* (i.e. there is no further new revelation), the idea of *fulness* is not brought out as clearly as in *Dei Verbum*.

There is, however, no mention of the interrelation between Israel and Christ within the general framework of revelation. The only hint of this is the reference to 'prophets and apostles'.[56] It is conceivable that this allusion to the two Testaments (even though they are not mentioned by name) is meant to convey the idea that within revelation are the elements of preparation and reality, or even prediction and fulfilment. This depends, however, on the view taken of prophecy, and of the New Testament use of the Old. Yet here again is either deficiency or vagueness.

iii) The *relation* between revelation and Scripture is summed up in the closing words of paragraph 42. They refer to the Bible as 'the treasure of the Word of God.' Revelation is associated with the Word of God, and the Bible is said to *contain* it. The Bible, therefore, is not to be regarded *in toto* as revelation.

The favourite concept used here is that of bearing witness — for example, 'to give witness to the revelation given'. Scripture is testimony, that is to say, a *human* testimony to revelation. Therefore, it is fallible. This is all of a piece with the view of revelation as personal and not propositional. It accords with the note struck by the progressive theologians in *Dei Verbum*.

Furthermore, the use of the word 'inaugurated' in the same paragraph is somewhat ambiguous in connection with the ministries of prophets and apostles. Giving it its best meaning, it would refer to their work as heralding God's self-revelation, each group doing so in its characteristic way. While this is unexceptionable, the word can conjure up the impression that, following them (and especially following the apostles), others continued the work as they did. The possibility of some kind of apostolic succession is here left open, particularly as it is the 'Tradition' of His revelation that is inaugurated. The Orthodox representatives would take that view. This also detracts from the uniqueness of the biblically presented relation between revelation and Scripture. In that relationship the latter is the unique, final and supremely authoritative inscripturation of the former.

2. Scripture and Inspiration

The statement about inspiration is inadequate. The word itself is used only in connection with a response to revelation, which is predicated equally of 'apostles and disciples'. Who are these disciples? Are they to be identified with the 'apostolic men' of *Dei Verbum* (those authors of New Testament books who were not themselves apostles)? Such an uncertainty should not be left in any reader's mind. We will consider both possibilities, as the consequences of each are serious.

If they were 'apostolic men', it will be seen from the statement that inspiration is extended only to them and not to their written testimony, as 2 Timothy 3:16 requires. Furthermore, the Scriptures were produced following the 'oral and written tradition of the prophets and apostles' and 'under the guidance of the Holy Spirit'.[57] This reference to the fact that traditions lie behind the Scriptural records indicates the recognition granted to oral tradition, source criticism and form criticism in New Testament studies. This contributes to the elevation of Tradition over Scripture in practical terms and, of course, it also projects the church to the fore.

If, on the other hand, the 'disciples' are ordinary Christians, then certain consequences follow as far as the doctrine of inspiration is concerned. 1 Corinthians 12:3 is quoted as a case of the inspiration of the Holy Spirit which is relevant to Scripture. But this means that His inspiration of Scripture is no different from His activity in engendering believing confession, because 1 Corinthians 12:3 refers to the declaration that 'Jesus is Lord'. This weakens the uniqueness of Scripture as God's verbalized expression of His mind and will in all its parts. 'Jesus is Lord' is our witness; Scripture is God's own witness. Inspiration cannot be reduced to 'the guidance of the Holy Spirit' as Montreal declares.

33

3. Scripture and Authority

This subject is a little more difficult to apprehend with confidence. The reason for this is not that the word 'authority' is absent from the text, nor is it because the need for such a concept fails to be recognized. In fact, a search *is* made for a criterion by which various traditions can be evaluated. It is rather because no precise answer is given to the question 'What is the ultimate authority?'

The clearest statement is that Scripture is 'regarded as the written prophetic and apostolic testimony to God's act in Christ, whose authority we all accept'.[58] This, however, does not really help, and that for two reasons. In the first place, the antecedent noun to the relative pronoun 'whose' is ambiguous. It could refer to Christ and not to Scripture at all. In the second place, even if it does refer to Scripture, its scope of reference is limited to 'God's act in Christ' as this is attested in Scripture. What parts of Scripture are these? We are not really set on clearly demarcated ground by this statement.

The use of the very formal word 'canonization' (para. 42 — see above, p.28) conveys the notion of the church — albeit under 'the guidance of the Spirit' — nevertheless bestowing something on the books of the two Testaments. What actually happened was that the church declared what books possessed authority in themselves. This notion of 'canonization' locates the Bible within the church in such a way that it cannot *really* be above the church. The influence of the Orthodox is visible here again. What we are arguing for is not that the Scripture is alone, but that it is *alone supreme*. It needs to be stated that, though the church (that is to say, the people of God) existed before the Bible was complete, the church from Sinai onwards was never without a partial and growing Bible. In addition, revelation was given orally before it was actually recorded, so God's people have *always* been under His Word.

TRADITION AND TRADITIONS

We must now turn to the subject of *Tradition* and *traditions*. The glossary, to which reference has already been made (see above p.28), must be our starting point. Paragraph 39 sets out these terms and their meanings:

In our report we have distinguished between a number of different meanings of the word *tradition*. We speak of the *Tradition* (with a capital T), *tradition* (with a small t) and *traditions*. By *the Tradition* is meant the Gospel itself, transmitted from generation to generation in and by the Church, Christ himself present in the life of the Church. By *tradition* is meant the traditionary process. The term *traditions* is used in two senses, to indicate both the diversity of forms of expression and also what we call confessional traditions, for instance the Lutheran tradition or the Reformed tradition. In the latter part of our report the word appears in a further sense, when we speak of cultural traditions.[59]

This paragraph shows the influence of the North American working group's report (see p.13), in which there are what are termed 'working definitions of hinge words'.[60] The members of this working group were church historians, and they came from the various church groupings within the WCC. As a result, they were well aware of the complexities of their assignment, whether it was viewed in its past or present manifestations. One of the difficulties they encountered was that the terminology, with which they were forced to work because it was essential to the subject and for which no alternative could be found, had neither a single nor a generally acceptable meaning for all concerned. Furthermore, these terms had polemical associations because of past controversies. That is why these 'working definitions' emerged, and they are essential for an understanding of the Montreal statement and subsequent ecumenical theology.

There is precise agreement between *Dei Verbum* and Montreal in the meanings they assign to 'the Tradition' and 'traditions', but there is a possible difference between them in their understanding of *tradition*. Montreal identifies *tradition* with 'the traditionary process'. The North American report says that it represents 'both the process of transmission . . . and also the substantive contents of whatever is transmitted'.[61] There seems to be more in the latter definition, but the working group's report then goes on to summarize the meaning of the term in the following words: 'It denotes the traditionary process operating in human history and society'. Does the Montreal definition include, therefore, the element of content as well as process? It would seem that it does so in at least one place. As a result, its definition is not as precise as it may at first appear. It speaks of 'the oral and written tradition of the prophets and apostles',[62]

35

and this cannot be restricted to process minus content. It would have been an easy matter to deal with this slight discrepancy. The fact that this was not done is an indication of how slippery the category differences, which have already been quoted, are.

In the remainder of this comment we shall consider what is said in the Montreal statement about each of these elements and, by so doing, throw into relief the nature of the crisis it had to face. We shall then examine some of the solutions which were proposed to deal with that crisis.

1. 'the Tradition'

The authors of the North American report, which lies behind the Montreal statement, make the revealing comment that this expression caused them grave difficulty. They stated the reason for their perplexity as follows: 'There is a doubt as to its proper use in critical historical parlance.'[63] This means that it is a fabricated term with no history worth mentioning in Christian theology. Those who adopted it justify what they have done by saying that it provides 'some sort of referent to which the plural traditions refer if they can be rightly classed as mutually related to each other.'[64] This, of course, begs the question as to whether all traditions are or can be rightly related — a point assumed here, but denied later when some traditions are deemed to be false. 'The Tradition' is an expression which serves a purpose without corresponding to any reality. It is functional and aims to turn a theory into a truth. It is 'ecumenical Newspeak'.[65] Well might the framers of the report be hesitant about it!

But they adopted it, and so did Montreal. It has, therefore, passed into ecumenism. And what is worse, this has been done in spite of the known fact that the term 'the Tradition' means different things to those who use it. It can mean 'the act of God in Christ', 'the work of the Spirit in salvation', 'the life of God in the Church', 'the Christian faith', 'the Holy Scriptures' and so on. To adopt a term which means different things to different people is an advantage only to those who are keen to outstrip Humpty Dumpty, who, when he used a word, used it to mean what *he* chose it to mean. At least *something* distinct was being spoken of in his parlance, even though it did not correspond with the proper meaning of the word. But in this report one word is a conglomerate, meaning not only one thing, but more than one — perhaps everything. This is desperate and it makes for confusion. Whatever the origin of the expression 'the Tradition', it is certainly not biblical. What is more, it is not Protestant. It is loaded in the direction of Roman Catholicism and Eastern Orthodoxy. Indeed, so powerful had the idea of Tradition become at Montreal that one section of the Conference proposed the following statement: 'We can say that we exist as Christians *sola traditione*, by tradition alone.'[66] This sentiment was shared by Protestant and Roman Catholic, but the statement was not approved for fear of its being misunderstood and offending those who upheld *sola Scriptura* — Scripture alone.[67]

In fact, the Montreal report is trying to claim that 'the Tradition' *cannot err.*

2. 'tradition'

This is the dynamic process by which 'the Tradition' is transmitted in and through the church. Included in this process are the following elements: '. . . the preaching of the Word, . . . the administration of the Sacraments and worship, . . . Christian teaching and theology, and . . . mission and witness to Christ by the lives of the members of the Church'.[68]

One may note the similarity between what is included in *tradition* and what *Dei Verbum* has to say about *Tradition*. J.P. Mackey plots the broad outline of the Roman Catholic view of *Tradition* as follows:

> They [i.e. Roman Catholic theologians] say that the notion of tradition has two essential elements. They call one the objective element and by that they mean to indicate the truth that is handed on. The second they call the subjective or active element and by that they indicate the process or activity of handing it on.[69]

For a Protestant, there is an inevitable conflict between the two elements, and it is doubtful if a third element could ever be found to remove the antithesis. It lies in Montreal's frankly expressed recognition that 'tradition can be a faithful transmission of the Gospel, but also a distortion of it'.[70] We read in the North American report that 'the traditionary process may operate in either direction, toward entropy or renewal.'[71] The crux of the matter is that *tradition* and its effects (namely, *traditions*) are not regarded as being inevitably good, in spite of the fact that they operate in and through the church. The possibility of the distortion of the Tradition, and of the disorder that would follow, is clearly envisaged. This is of course a testimony to the continuing influence of the Protestant Reformation. It amounts to the assertion that *tradition can err*.

3. 'traditions'

This term designates the various concrete *forms* actually taken by the traditionary *process* (e.g. denominations, confessions, liturgies, polities, etc.). These 'proliferate endlessly' and 'exhibit great diversity'.[72] Concerning all these as they appear in the younger churches and in the West, and throughout the past, Montreal says: 'The traditions in Christian history are distinct from, and yet connected with, the Tradition. They are the expressions and manifestations in diverse historical forms of the one truth and reality which is Christ'.[73]

This concentration upon traditions in relation to Tradition is what most of all distinguishes Montreal from *Dei Verbum*. In the latter reference is made to Tradition in general terms. Its forms are not mentioned. F.C. Grant states in his response to *Dei Verbum* (published in *The Documents of Vatican II*):[74]

> If only the Constitution had said something about the claims made for such doctrines as the Assumption of the Blessed Virgin, as based upon sound tradition, it would have clarified the minds of many inquirers. And it might have started a 'dialogue' destined to open the whole question of the criteria of true tradition, and the tests by which extra-biblical teaching should be re-evaluated.[75]

This is, of course, a Protestant outlook. At this point, for the Roman Catholic, the role of the magisterium and the idea of doctrinal development come in, and the existence of the problem is denied. The Protestant, however, must affirm (as, indeed, Montreal does) that *traditions can be false* — that is, not genuine.

To make such an affirmation is to produce a problem of great magnitude. This arises out of the facts which have already been confessed, namely, that tradition can err and that resultant traditions can be false. They remain untrue despite whatever legitimate connection may be claimed for them with the Tradition which cannot err. The unavoidable question Montreal had to raise was: 'How can we distinguish between traditions embodying the true Tradition and merely human traditions? Where do we find the genuine Tradition, and where impoverished tradition or even distortion of tradition?'[76]

The Montreal report provides an answer with regard both to traditions which exist and those which are likely to come into being (i.e. in the missionary context). The third main section deals with the latter under the heading 'The Christian Tradition and Cultural Diversity'. The emergence of false traditions is to be prevented by application of a threefold resolve, namely:

> 1. To adhere to what is 'basic in the Old and New Testament record and interpretation' in dependence on the 'leading' of the Holy Spirit, and with an awareness of God's 'providential operations' in the world.

> 2. To refuse to admit (into the life of the church, one assumes) anything 'which is at variance with the good news of what God has done, is doing and will do, in the redemption of the world through our Lord Jesus Christ, as expressed in terms of the Church's christocentric and trinitarian faith'.

> 3. To transmit the whole of God's truth (i.e. 'the Tradition in its fulness') and not to over-emphasize 'those elements which are especially congenial to a particular culture'.[77]

However fine they may sound, it must be seriously doubted whether these guidelines will prove adequate to achieve the desired end. They are so vague. What is 'basic in the Old and New Testament record' is not specified, much less what is basic in its interpretation. Furthermore, who decides what comes into this category is a question which is left open. And what constitutes 'the redemption of the world'? This is a subject often debated in current theology and action. Because these guidelines contain such ambiguities and uncertainties, they cannot prevent very diverse and even conflicting traditions from coming into being in the future. In addition, to combine the leading of the Spirit with the providential activity of God is probably to confuse them.

But what of already existing traditions? How can these be evaluated? The second section of the report, which is entitled 'The Unity of Tradition and the Diversity of Traditions', suggests that what is required is a new way of studying the histories of the various communions — 'a study of history which is ecumenical in its scope and spirit'.[78]

This is a reflection of the North American report, in which the authors make the following contention: 'There is in church history a corollary to the principle of historical relativism in general historiography' — that is, an idealized view of one's own religious traditions. Leaving 'partisan history' and focusing on 'that history which Christians have in common by virtue of the historical existence of the Church and the life of faith', it is said that 'a new understanding of some of the most contested areas of our common past'[79] will emerge. This is 'ecumenical historiography', the writing up of history (particularly disagreements and controversies) from the standpoint of present-day ecumenism.

In response, it needs to be said that if contending for one's tradition can lead to a partisan view, so an emphasis on oneness can lead to a minimizing or overlooking of the differences. The Anglican-Roman Catholic International Commission's statement on justification is proof of this. The same is true of that body's treatment of Scripture. No reference is made to the disagreements over the sufficiency and perspicuity of Scripture, that is, whether or not Scripture needs to be supplemented and interpreted by the tradition — in some cases the *authoritative* tradition — of the church. Tradition is given a real if restricted independence of Scripture (see para. 2: 'Authority in the Church: Elucidation' in *The Final Report*). This new way of approaching history is not the solution its devotees imagine it to be.[80] It will not supply the criterion to distinguish true from false.

We must now turn to the first main section of the Montreal statement, which is entitled 'Scripture, Tradition and Traditions'. Here the need for a criterion is recognized and confessed, and an attempt is made to discover one (paras. 49-55). It is to the New Testament that the report immediately turns in this search, and describes it as '*an* indispensable criterion'.[81] The indefinite article is not in italic script in the original text, but we have used italics to draw attention to the fact that the New Testament is not regarded as sufficient by itself. The truth of this can be seen in the way the report proceeds to speak of the fact and necessity of the church's interpretation of the New Testament. To that, however, must be added the variety of such interpretations. Therefore, the criteriological problem — the search for a

40

criterion to distinguish false from true — is not only *compounded* by a hermeneutical one (the search for the right interpretation), but it is thereby *rendered insoluble*.

As a result of being unable to affirm for differing reasons that Scripture is inerrant, or that the Church (magisterium) is 'indefectible' (Küng's term), there exists no single criterion adequate for the purpose of evaluating traditions. The Montreal report, therefore, takes the position that the needed standard is composed both of Scripture and the church. This is what the Orthodox believe and what Rome teaches. The Montreal report has no place for the *sola Scriptura* of the Reformation. This means that the Reformation challenge to Rome is equally applicable to the Ecumenical Movement.

In the preceding pages, we have attempted to examine the breakthrough made at Montreal over the controversial question of how Scripture and Tradition are to be related. In doing so, we have sought to be as descriptive and as impartial as possible.

It must now be made clear that the breakthrough was not made in terms of the original conflict and its basic issue. That issue was whether Holy Scripture was sufficient and clear to teach the truth and rule the church **by itself** (*sola Scriptura*) — that is, without anything being added to it from any other source, within as well as outside the church. In the Montreal statement that issue is not raised or addressed. And it is in that statement rather than *Dei Verbum* that one is entitled to see it, because it is a Protestant conviction. Yet, at best, it is overlooked. The breakthrough, then, is then not a *real* one in terms of the original dispute which is enshrined in the confessions.

The breakthrough has instead been achieved in terms of what is being thought today about Scripture and Tradition. What is more, it has been achieved by a *deus ex machina*. A *deus ex machina* is a character invented by a playwright. This character is introduced without warning at the end of a play to solve the problem created by the plot — a problem which the author could not resolve by using the characters already at his disposal. It is a measure of an author's failure.

The Tradition is an ecumenical *deus ex machina* of a verbal kind. It is a way of resolving the head-on clash between Holy Scripture and church tradition. It avoids the grim reality of the conflict. *The Tradition* includes both, and therefore gives the victory to each.

But is that what is accomplished? Does Holy Scripture come out of this reconstruction as a *real* victor? The use of the term 'tradition' for the overarching concept or reality, in which Scripture is given a place — whatever that place may be — argues against this being the case. Whatever the origin and lineage of the term 'the Tradition' may be, it is certainly not a Protestant way of speaking. It leans in a Catholic direction and favours the church rather than the Bible. It is therefore capable of integration with Roman Catholicism and potentially destructive not only of Protestantism but also of Christianity itself.

THE BREACH

From the standpoint of ecumenism, a *breakthrough* was achieved at Montreal with regard to the Scripture-Tradition conflict. At the same time, however, there was also a *breach* with the view of the Bible which had previously held sway in WCC theology. That view was not the orthodox (evangelical) view of the Scriptures. Evangelicals maintain that the Bible is in all its parts inspired ('breathed out') by God and consequently infallible or inerrant in all that it teaches. Such a doctrine has never been the hallmark of twentieth-century theology, and this is reflected in the ARCIC statements. In the latter, *revelation* is only personal; it is not propositional. *Inspiration* is not verbal, and *infallibility* can only be predicated of God. To describe Scripture as a 'normative record' means no more than a 'written standard', and even 'a primary norm' is not the same as 'the supreme rule'.

At Montreal the breach was made with the view of the Bible espoused by the biblical theology movement. This is a twentieth-century school of thought, which works on the basis of the neo-orthodox theology of Karl Barth and Emil Brunner. The Wadham College statement, to which reference has been made, is an excellent example of this kind of approach to the Bible. Hans-Ruedi Weber, the current Director of the World Council's Portfolio on Biblical Studies, has described this approach as follows: 'The biblical theology movement is marked by the combination of a critical approach to the Bible with a confessing theology, emphasising the unity of the Bible and its witness to the history of salvation.'[82]

A symposium of essays, which arose out of the Wadham College conference and expounded its findings, was later published. It was entitled *Biblical Authority for Today*.[83] It was at the New Delhi Assembly of the WCC that this outlook on the Bible reached the peak of its influence. There Dr Visser't Hooft, a leading exponent of this theology and General Secretary of the WCC from 1948 to 1966, declared that it was the Bible which gave the WCC its marching orders. The New Delhi statements repeatedly use the expression 'the biblical understanding' with reference to the various subjects it considered, e.g. reconciliation and service.[84] It was, of course, at New Delhi that the WCC's basis of membership was enlarged to include a reference to the Scriptures as well as to the Trinity.[85]

As a result, therefore, of regarding both Testaments as having Christ as their centre, and being accounts of God's saving acts in history for His people, it seemed that, in spite of a rejection of the infallibility of the Bible, the WCC had a generally accepted view of Scripture for its base. But this was all to change at Montreal.

The collapse in the view of the Bible which has just been described was brought about by statements which were grounded on the same critical view of the Bible which the biblical theology movement had never repudiated. The force of these statements could not, therefore, be denied. They had the effect of showing that the themes of salvation-history, which were thought to integrate the Bible, were not supported by biblical exegesis of a higher critical kind.

It was probably Ernst Käsemann's address at Montreal which lit the touch paper. His subject was 'Unity and Diversity in New Testament Ecclesiology'. In this he exploded the notion that the New Testamant taught a *single* view of the church. He declared:

> No romantic postulate, dressed up as *Heilsgeschichte*, can relativize the sober fact that the historian simply cannot speak of an unbroken unity of New Testament ecclesiology, for he perceives there the early pattern of our situation, with its differences, dilemmas and antitheses.[86]

Another speaker, Raymond E. Brown, a Roman Catholic scholar, concurred with this, but sought to contend for the presence of some common elements amid this diversity: for example, the apostles' role and the sacraments. Käsemann's thesis aroused many fears for the future of the Ecumenical Movement, particularly among the elder statesmen of the WCC. 'One church' no longer seemed an attainable goal.

Flesseman-van Leer lists the following items as consequences of the breach which we have been describing. She writes:

> It seems impossible to speak univocally any more of *the* biblical message, or *the* biblical doctrine in respect of a particular issue. The importance of critical biblical scholarship was affirmed and the insight that the use of this exegetical tool had far-reaching *theological* consequences was brought home [italics original].[87]

Given such an acknowledgement of diversity in the Bible, the questions of its interpretation and authority were inevitably raised. Ever since Montreal these have been the main subjects on Faith and Order Conference agenda. Interpretation was dealt with at Bristol in 1967, and authority at Louvain in 1971. A particular nexus of these themes was dealt with at Bangalore in 1977, namely, the relation between the two Testaments. We shall briefly survey these subjects and try to see where the Ecumenical Movement is going with regard to the Bible.

INTERPRETATION

The powerful influence which confessional traditions exerted on member churches as they sought to interpret Scripture was recognized at Montreal. In addition, different 'keys' were used by the churches in their interpretative study — for example:

- the analogy of faith
- the 'centre' of Scripture (i.e. its main theme — no one theme was agreed on by all who looked at Scripture in this way)
- the individual conscience
- the mind of the church
- the deposit of faith
- the magisterium

These differences in methodology were bound to lead to diversity of conclusions. In the light of such variety, the Montreal report raised the question, 'How can we overcome the situation in which we all read Scripture in the light of our own traditions?'[88] The answer given to this question is that the Tradition should be sought by *corporate* study of the Bible and study of the Fathers of *all periods of the Church's history* but 'in the light

44

of our ecumenical task'.[89] Clearly, there is an ongoing search for an ecumenical hermeneutic to match ecumenical historiography! The result of this is hardly likely to be the hearing of the authentic Word of God.

Other influences are being brought to bear on the hermeneutical enterprise beside the ecumenical one. Two of these call for notice and comment.

The human character of Scripture

The first of these is the almost total preoccupation with the humanness of Scripture. Evangelicals have always doubted whether the divine character of Scripture was being properly acknowledged in ecumenical theology, in spite of the many references to its being the Word of God. Now, however, the pendulum is very definitely at the other extreme. In contrasting the Wadham and Bristol statements, Flesseman-van Leer points out that the former begins with positive theological presuppositions, while the latter is conspicuously lacking in this regard. In addition, the Bristol report denies the validity and applicability of any one interpretative principle as 'a prescriptive instrument applicable in all circumstances'. Only 'provisional principles of interpretation' are allowed, and then only because one needs to begin somehow. If there is no certainty about the character of the Bible nor about its interpretation, then the only certain thing about its study in an ecumenical context is that its conclusions are totally uncertain. Flesseman-van Leer writes:

> The Bristol report makes no reference whatever to theological presuppositions; the exegetical process which it describes is in the main valid equally for both biblical and other literary documents. In the first and most specific section, dealing with hermeneutics, the consensus presented is dominated by the acknowledgement that the Bible is a collection of *human* writings [italics original].[90]

An influential figure in the discussions at Bristol and Louvain was James Barr.[91] He analyzed and summarized the findings of study groups set up following Montreal, and these were incorporated in the report which was presented at the Bristol conference. He performed the same sort of task for a consultation on authority set up after Bristol for the conference at Louvain. Barr's position on Scripture is well known. It includes the frank admission of error in Scripture as a necessary part of its humanness. He locates the authority of Scripture in its role or function rather than in its character. These views are expressed in the statements which received the approval of the Bristol and Louvain conferences.

Diversity within Scripture

The second influence derives from the diversity present in the Bible — one which brings its human character to a sharp focus. What is the nature of this diversity? Is it not the case that diversity has always been regarded as a characteristic of the biblical record? If by diversity no more is meant than a striking and rich variety, then that, of course, is true. But more than that is meant by this particular use of the term. The Bristol report, which bears the title *The Significance of the Hermeneutical Problem for the Ecumenical Movement*, declares: 'The Bible contains a collection of very diverse literary traditions, the contents of which often stand *in tension* with one another' (italics mine).[92]

What kind of tension is this? While admitting that some differences may be 'complementary aspects of the truth', the report states: 'Sometimes, as far as we can see, there may be real contradictions . . . [such] diversities and contradictions should not be glossed over . . . [and] it is essential that forced harmonization should be avoided.'[93]

Examples of such contradictions are given. They are:

> . . . the concept of providence in the Chronicles and the book of Job [and] the way in which the future of Israel is conceived in 1 Thessalonians 2:14-16 and Romans 11:25ff. Even Christological statements in the New Testament are sometimes in tension, compare e.g. Romans 1:3ff and Matthew 1:18ff and John 1:1ff.[94]

Though the report recognizes that such admissions have a knock-on effect for the authority of the Bible, there does not seem to be any concern, let alone alarm about this, in spite of the confession that these contradictions are not superficial. Barr talks openly about 'a possibly basic theological disagreement'[95] existing in the Bible. By the word 'basic' is meant what the Bristol report refers to as 'real theological disagreements within the Biblical period itself. Such disagreements are to be found in the earliest form of the written text.'[96] This means that no hope can be entertained of peeling away layers of tradition which interpret an earlier form of the text so as to arrive at a text free of contradictions. This is most serious. It is to enthrone contradiction in the place of consistency and to deny that unity of truth is to be found in Holy Scripture. Given such a view, what hope can there be for unity in truth in the church?

However, ecumenists see real gain in viewing Scripture in this way because it immediately has the effect of reducing the grim reality of their own divided state. Instead of viewing their divisions as something to be overcome by resolution, it is now possible to see them in the Bible. The diversity of the churches is rooted in the diversity of Scripture. The Bristol report says:

> The diversity of thought within the Bible reflects the diversity of God's actions in different historical situations and the diversity of human response to God's actions . . . There is a diversity of church traditions which in some of its aspects may be related to that diversity of traditions already found in the Bible.[97]

Toward the end of the report we read:

> The awareness of the differences within the Bible will lead us towards a deeper understanding of our divisions and will help us to interpret them more readily as possible and legitimate interpretations of one and the same Gospel.[98]

This view of the Bible has the effect of closing the gap between one interpretation of Scripture and the traditions present in the churches. Having rejected one kind of 'forced harmonization', the pressure is on for another kind of the same. More seriously, Scripture loses its independent status and critical role over the church. How can Scripture possibly function as a theological criterion when it is itself theologically contradictory? If Scripture legitimizes the diversity in the churches, how can real unity be achieved? More seriously, how can the real truth be known?

AUTHORITY

One's view of the Bible's character has inevitable consequences for one's view of its authority. This was acknowledged in the Bristol conference, and so the subject was delegated to its successor. If the Bible is not held to be infallible in its teaching, and that is what the claim to find contradictions in it amounts to, then it cannot be irrefragable in its authority. James Barr readily acknowledges the possible need to make 'a choice within the totality of the Bible'[99] in order that theological interpretation might proceed. This means at least excluding some biblical material from consideration. But who will make such a choice? And on what basis? Excluding Scripture alone, the only options are an ecumenical council, an infallible Pope or magisterium, or a consensus among biblical scholars. Infallibility is an inescapable concept. The debate is over *where* it is to be located and *how* it is to be described. In other words, is infallibility the mark of the Bible, the church or tradition?

What did Louvain have to say on the authority of the Bible? We must draw attention to two matters. The first of these concerns which books have authority, and the second has to do with the kind of authority they possess.

The Extent of the Canon

The question of the biblical canon was one which had not been faced directly by the Faith and Order Movement. There was, however, an awareness that it could not be avoided forever. Following the Bristol conference, James Barr noted that attention needed to be given to it, because disagreement existed over what should be interpreted. While some regarded the books of the Bible as a basic source, others saw them only as one expression among others of Christian truth. The delegates at Louvain decided to extend whatever authority biblical books possess to other literature. The relevant statement is:

> The dividing line between canonical and non-canonical writings is not a hard and fast one. It is much more a matter of a fluid boundary. As we have already said, even the witnesses included in the canon do not have the same significance.[100]

This statement brackets apocryphal (and perhaps pseudepigraphical) literature with biblical writings. Having said this, the Louvain document immediately proceeds to try to retain something unique for the canonical books, but it is able to do this only on the basis that the church recognizes the Bible as special. But which church is being referred to? And, by implication, whose Bible? The Roman Catholic Church and the Protestant churches disagree over the extent of the canon, but ARCIC does not face this matter. In opening the canon, Louvain had taken a further step in the direction of weakening the Scripture.

The Kind of Authority

In October 1968, a Faith and Order Consultation was held at Böldern near Zürich. It reflected on the Bristol conference and did preparatory work for Louvain. Its findings and suggestions were summarized by James Barr. The consultation recommended that, in future, any consideration of the authority of the Bible should be approached '*not* by a directly dogmatic method and *not* by a general consideration of biblical authority abstracted from the exegetical situation, but by the interpretation of particular biblical passages in their relation to a chosen theme' (italics original).[101] Several reasons were given for the adoption of this approach, including the following: 'A general or dogmatic approach is likely to pass by the problem of the *diversity* of the Bible and the questions of authority posed by it.'[102] Clearly, any view of the Bible's authority which emerged from studies which rejected the presence of contradictions in the Bible would not be acceptable to the Ecumenical Movement. This was to outlaw the infallible authority of the Bible as an ecumenical option. The consultation listed several interesting theological questions for study, but the above quotation makes it clear that they were all to be considered from within the framework of the Bible's diversity as defined. The scales were loaded.

Given the emphasis on the Bible's human character and its diversity, it was inevitable that authority would be located somewhere other than in the Scriptures alone. *Sola Scriptura* came to be regarded as an impossibility in the modern context. It was at best an archaism as far as ecumenism was concerned.

What then was Louvain's view of the Bible's authority? There is no single, straightforward answer to this question. Louvain's view of the subject is made up of three elements. The first is that the Bible has 'a certain weight as a literary document', i.e. it exists as an object. The second is that it is 'the oldest documentation of the apostolic message' and, as such, it is an unavoidable point of reference of some kind for the church. It is the third element which states the distinctive view of authority for which Louvain is known, namely, that the authority of the Bible is a 'relational concept.'[103] What is meant by this is unfolded in the following words: 'When we speak of the "authority" of the Bible in the strict sense, we mean that it makes the Word of God audible and is therefore able to lead men to faith.'[104]

49

The Anglican-Roman Catholic International Commission (ARCIC) operates with the same view of the authority of the Bible. *The Final Report* of the Commission declares: 'Through these written words the authority of the Word of God is conveyed.'[105] This says something about the *effect* of Scripture but not its nature. The sentence which we have just quoted does not mean the same as the following sentence: 'In these written words the authority of the Word of God is found.'

There is, of course, no debate over whether the Bible *does* make its authority felt in this way, nor is there any dispute about the fact that when it does so, it is *God's* authority which is made known. What is troubling is that the authority of the Bible should be defined *primarily* in this way. This statement raises the question of whether the Bible's authority cannot be defined in relation to itself, i.e. what it is, as distinct from what it does. We propose two tests to determine whether Louvain takes this functional view of authority. The first is what this statement has to say about the Bible itself, and the second is what it has to say about the Bible and unbelief.

The Bible itself

If we were to claim that the relational/functional view of the Bible's authority is in itself destructive of the Bible's uniqueness, it would be hotly disputed. In support of that view of biblical authority it would be pointed out that Louvain emphasizes the Bible's 'otherness'. The all-important statement is probably the following: 'Authority is therefore a present reality only when men experience it as authority; at the same time, it transcends human experience. Special and explicit emphasis must be placed on this supra-individual character of authority [Section IV].'[106] It would be claimed that this states all that is necessary with regard to what the Bible is. But does it?

In the first sentence just quoted, the heavier emphasis is on the first part. For all its transcendence, authority is only a reality when men recognize it to be so. This leads to the second question we shall consider, namely, 'Is it authoritative when men do *not* recognize it to be so?' The answer to that question will say something about the kind of transcendence the Bible possesses.

As will be noted, the second sentence concludes with a reference to another section of the Louvain report where the 'supra-individual character of authority' presumably receives 'special and explicit emphasis.' This section is entitled 'Holy Spirit, Church and Inspiration'. The key word in this section for the view of authority which it presents is the word 'prove'. We read: 'What we mean [by authority] is . . . that through the Bible God proves himself to be the Lord and the Redeemer . . . The content of the Bible must prove itself authoritative.'[107]

This statement reasserts the relational view and still does not speak of what the Bible is in itself. We must couple with these statements the way that other attempts to speak of the Bible's authority — on the basis of its unique message, and on the basis of its being the source of faith in the Church over the ages — are rejected by Louvain. In addition, the 'traditional view' of inspiration is rejected as the basis of the Bible's authority. This is because it is 'a dogma whose validity is presupposed'. It is as if 2 Timothy 3:16, 2 Peter 1:21 and (in consequence) John 10:35 are not in the Bible. However, inspiration cannot be totally disregarded because of the logic of the Bible's efficacy, and so a particular kind of inspiration is posited. What kind? Just as the 'relational' model predominates in the case of authority, so it does with inspiration. We read:

> If we speak here of inspiration, it is important to observe the fundamental difference between this use and the traditional doctrine of inspiration. What in the latter is a dogmatic assumption is here the outcome of the experience in which the message of the Bible proves itself authoritative.[108]

From all this it should be clear that it is no longer possible or even acceptable in ecumenism to speak of the Bible, its inspiration and authority, as a thing *by itself*. Some connection must always be made, it seems, between the Bible and the church, or between the Bible and the individual in terms of recognition and interpretation. This means that, in practice, it is inevitable that the Bible will not be given its place and role as the suprahuman and supra-ecclesiastical Word of God.

The Bible and Unbelief

It is, of course, the experiencing of the Bible's message as applied by the Holy Spirit which leads one to believe that it is the Word of God. But there lies an important point of theological distinction. It concerns the difference between *what the Bible is* and *how it is perceived to be what it is*. That distinction has been erased by this report, if it was ever considered, and as a result, it has become impossible to speak of the Bible apart from the individual believer or the church.

This situation is reinforced by another factor. Nothing at all is said about the fact that the Bible is not being perceived for what it is and the bearing which this has on the authority it is declared to possess. If authority, even supra-human authority, has to be *perceived* to be authority to qualify as authoritative, then 'no effect — no authority' is not an unfair presentation of Louvain's view of the Bible. But *is* it the Bible's own view of itself? Is it not rather the case that God's Word spoken or written *is* God's Word, whether men will hear or forbear, or whether they believe or reject it? To fail to speak thus of the Bible is to fail to speak *properly* of the Bible, whatever else we may say about it.

*　　*　　*　　*　　*　　*

We have been describing a struggle — a struggle between church (ecumenism) and Bible. Vatican II was at great pains to give something more to the Bible in terms of prominence *vis-à-vis* the church than had formerly appeared to be the case. The Montreal delegates, who consisted of those who were neither Roman Catholics nor Eastern Orthodox, were anxious to speak more positively about the church *vis-à-vis* the Bible than had been done before. The preceding pages indicate something of the difficulties they all encountered — and, of course, the story has not ended.

But a point has been reached where evangelicals can take stock. How has the Bible fared in all this? There is only one answer that an evangelical can give to that question. It is that the Bible has lost out — and lost out to the church.

When 'the Tradition' terminology was adopted at Montreal, Scripture became totally 'ecclesiasticized' — that is to say, it was brought within the orbit of the church. As a result, it became notionally impossible for the Bible ever to be detached from the church so as to be above her. It also became practically impossible for the Scriptures to be regarded in that way, because it would have meant a recognition of the Bible as the supreme judge of the church in all her affairs. The magisterium of the Roman Catholic Church and the 'Christ in the Church' of the Eastern Orthodox churches therefore remained intact.

When the relational view of inspiration and authority was accepted, the Bible became thoroughly 'humanized'. It became a human record about God, errant in parts, which was to be evaluated and endorsed by human beings and interpreted by them. The church was involved in these areas, because such activities could take place properly only in the church and by the Spirit in the church. It came to be believed that the Holy Spirit was no more opposed to ecumenism than Holy Scripture was. The Bible had become first and last 'the document of the faith of the Church',[109] but it was no longer in reality 'the revealed, inspired and inerrant Word of God.'

In fact, the church has emasculated the Bible. *Sola ecclesia* or *sola Traditione* has replaced *sola Scriptura*.

2
The Death of Christ

At Whitsuntide 1982 the mass was presented to the British public as never before. This was, of course, the direct result of the open-air masses concelebrated by Pope John Paul II and others during his visit to Britain and the degree of television coverage given to that visit. However, the distinctive and essential nature of the Roman Catholic mass was itself obscured by the remarks of the imperceptive broadcasters and the use of the technical terms *mystery* and *eucharist*. One of the aims of this chapter is to concentrate our attention on what was then either overlooked or omitted, namely transubstantiation and its significance.

But why should such a thing be attempted at all? It is not merely that the record should be put straight. Nor is that even the main purpose. Our concern is rather that what was not brought to the fore then should now be examined because of its importance not only for Roman Catholicism but also for Christianity. The mass is the centre of Roman Catholic worship. It can even be regarded as a miniature of the most distinctive features of Roman Catholicism itself. Even more important than this, however, is the claim that is made by the Roman Catholic Church concerning the relationship between the mass and the death of the Lord Jesus Christ. This is that the mass possesses a most intimate connection with the significance and continuing efficacy of the death of the Lord on Calvary. As this death is, according to the testimony of the apostles in the New Testament, the sum and substance of genuine Christianity, there is an important link between the mass and Christianity itself.

It is therefore of the utmost importance that the nature of this connection be investigated and evaluated so that a decision may be made about its validity. In doing this, we shall also be involved in assessing the worth of Roman Catholicism as a whole. This is because several of its most cherished features find concentrated expression in the mass — for example: the nature and role of the priesthood, the nature of faith and the means of grace. The relationship between the mass and the cross is therefore not only an important subject in itself, but one which is fraught with the most far-reaching consequences for the Christian, for the church and for Christianity itself.

It is recognized that the nature and aim of this chapter run counter to the broad consensus of religious opinion here in Britain. This majority seeks to promote what will bring professing Christians closer together by concentrating on what they seem to have in common and by deferring (at least for the time being) any real consideration of the differences between them. To focus on differences between religious communions, and especially on those doctrines which have always been a source of controversy in the past is, so these people would argue, bound to put off further the day of a single and universal Christian Church. After all, a divided Christendom dishonours Christ. It invites and merits the scorn of our increasingly secular society. People will therefore feel that the contents of a chapter like this will be to the detriment of both the church herself and her influence in the world. What is more, the argument continues, it will be a kind of return to the sixteenth century, the era of doctrinal conflict and church division. It might also give the impression to non-religious folk that the situation and atmosphere between the churches is no different today from what it was then.

Obviously, there are several features of the outlook just described which demand some comment, if only by way of justification of this study. Such comment, however, will serve to introduce its content. First, it must be remembered that there is a relationship between the church and doctrine. The church is 'the pillar and ground of the truth'.[1] Secondly, the church which does not speak plainly and confidently about what it believes and what it rejects neither merits nor receives the respect of society. Thirdly, while it is true that the mass was a matter of fierce controversy between *theologians* in the sixteenth century, it needs to be appreciated that *ordinary* people at that time felt the matter was crucial and that the truth was something dear enough to die for. The realization of this fact should go at least some way toward countering the idea that theologians of four centuries later (i.e. our own day) can with real justification treat this subject as if it were a mere matter of words. The issues inherent in the mass dare not be circumvented in that way. So, any claim that agreement has now been reached between the descendants of those who disagreed so strongly in the sixteenth century must be examined carefully.

This, then, is what we have to do. We must look at Roman Catholic teachings about the mass and examine their bearing on the New Testament teaching regarding the cross of the Lord Jesus Christ. But this must be done in today's situation. In particular, it must be done in the light of the claim made by the members of the Anglican-Roman Catholic International Commission (ARCIC) in their *Final Report* to 'have reached agreement on essential points of eucharistic doctrine'.[2]

THE MASS

What then does the Roman Catholic Church teach concerning the mass? To answer this question properly two distinctions must first be made and clearly understood.

1. *There is a distinction to be made between what the Roman Catholic Church teaches and what certain Roman Catholic theologians are saying.*

Of late, some very striking things have been said by some Roman Catholic theologians. The Second Vatican Council summoned by Pope John XXIII gave a tremendous boost to many liberals, progressive priests and theologians to present and argue for changes in Roman Catholicism. Some unexpected utterances were made both at the Council and subsequent to it. Most notable among these progressive thinkers is Hans Küng, a professor of theology at Tübingen University. Küng's licence to teach as an approved theologian of the Church was revoked by John Paul II because of the views he was propounding. Küng has attacked the idea of papal infallibility,[3] has rejected the term 'priest' and sees the Roman Catholic Church as being in danger of making mediators between God and men.[4] He says that 'the Mass and the other six sacraments of the Roman Catholic Church as a sacramental scheme are a product of history unknown during the first thousand years, presented for the first time in the twelfth century'.[5]

Now here is the point which must be made and understood: however much Protestants may like the sound of these and similar comments, it would be quite wrong to regard them as official Roman Catholic teaching. For that we must look elsewhere. The fact that Küng was censured is proof of this. Roman Catholic teaching is to be found in the decrees of general councils and in statements made by the Pope when he means to define a matter of faith or morals for the faithful. It is to this teaching that we must turn for an answer to our question.

2. *Another distinction which needs to be made is between what the Roman Catholic Church teaches about the mass and certain changes which have been introduced in that religious service.*

The Second Vatican Council, which met from 1960 to 1965, approved the introduction of certain significant changes in the service of the mass. One of these was that the mass no longer needed to be celebrated in Latin, but the language of the people could be used. In addition to this, there were also the following alterations, namely: increased use of Scripture for the purposes of public reading, greater emphasis on the homily or address, more participation in the service by the people, and even the granting of a theoretical possibility that people might be allowed by the Pope and the bishop to take bread *and wine* on certain specific occasions. All these are to be found in the Council's promulgation entitled 'The Constitution of the Sacred Liturgy'.[6]

Yet in spite of all these and other changes, the official teaching concerning the significance of the mass has remained the same. In 'The Constitution on the Sacred Liturgy' we find the following:

> The rite of the Mass is to be revised in such a way that the intrinsic nature and purpose of its several parts, as well as the connection between them, may be more clearly manifested, and that devout and active participation by the faithful may be more easily achieved. For this purpose the rites are to be simplified, *due care being taken* to preserve their substance [italics mine].[7]

And further, and most important:

> The dogmatic principles which were laid down by the Council of Trent remaining intact . . .[8]

58

These statements indicate that what has taken place in the Roman Catholic Church with regard to the mass can best be described to Protestants as 'changes in the order of service' but not in the significance of its essentials. What the dogma of the Second Vatican Council indicates is that the dogma of the Council of Trent on the meaning of the mass is still valid and determinative of its significance today.

The Council of Trent, which met from 1545 to 1563, was summoned mainly to deal with the disputes caused by the Protestant Reformation. The promulgations which relate to the subject of the mass were formulated in the seventh, thirteenth, twenty-first and twenty-second sessions of the Council.[9] It is to these documents that we now turn for an answer to the question: 'What does the Roman Catholic Church teach about the Mass?'

The dogma of the Roman Catholic Church regarding the mass can be summed up in the following statements:

1. The mass is not only a sacrament, but is also (and primarily) a sacrifice.
2. The mass is a sacrifice of the body and blood of Christ.

We shall consider each in turn.

1. THE MASS IS A SACRIFICE

The Mass is not only a sacrament; it is a sacrifice as well. This is asserted by Pope John Paul II in his encyclical letter, *The Mystery and Worship of the Holy Eucharist* (1980), as follows: 'The Eucharist is above all else a sacrifice'.[10]

It is this sacrificial element which not only differentiates the mass from the Lord's supper, but also distinguishes it from the other six sacraments of the Roman Catholic Church which are not sacrifices.

What, then, is the difference between a sacrament and a sacrifice? This is a most important matter. A *sacrament* is a visible sign or symbol, a visible pledge or promise of grace presented to people by God in spite of their sin. A *sacrifice* is a visible token presented by priests to God to obtain grace for people because of their sin. The movement of a *sacrament* is downward; it is from God to people. The movement of a *sacrifice* is upward; it is from people to God.

In the mass, therefore, something is being offered to God for sin. This is a basic and constituent element of the mass and the Roman Catholic Church is still committed to it. The Council of Trent says: 'If anyone shall say that in the mass a true and real sacrifice is not offered to God . . . let him be accursed (anathema sit)'.[11]

Much has recently been said about the mass as a sacrament which can include participation by the people in praise and petition. Great emphasis has been placed on this kind of participation. The faithful can even distribute the host to each other. It is clear, however, that in addition to such changes, some unauthorized changes have gone too far. One effect of this was that the sacrificial element became obscured. The papal encyclical of 1980, *The Mystery and Worship of the Holy Eucharist*, therefore sought to check this. John Paul II wrote that the words of the *celebrant* — 'pray that my sacrifice and yours may be acceptable to God, the Almighty Father' — are '*binding* since they express the character of the entire Eucharistic liturgy and the fulness of its divine and ecclesial content' (italics mine).[12]

This, then, is one of the points which must claim our attention as we examine the ARCIC statement. Does that statement repudiate or accept the language of sacrifice in relation to the eucharist? Historically, this is what the Roman Catholic Church asserts and what Protestantism originally rejected. We shall answer this question after the next point which is inseparably joined to this matter of sacrifice.

2. THE MASS IS A SACRIFICE OF THE BODY AND BLOOD OF CHRIST

We have seen how the element of sacrifice is essential to the mass. We must go further than this, however, and observe that the sacrifice, which is the mass, is nothing less than an offering of the body and blood of the Lord. The Council of Trent declares:

> First of all, the Holy Council teaches and openly and plainly professes that after the consecration of bread and wine our Lord Jesus Christ, true God and true man, is *truly, really* and *substantially* contained in the august sacrament of the Holy Eucharist under the appearance of those sensible things [italics mine].[13]

These three terms '*truly, really* and *substantially*' refer to a reality which is qualitatively different from the highest degree of symbolic representation. Canon 1 of Session XIII of the Council of Trent declares:

> If anyone shall deny that in the sacrament of the most Holy Eucharist are contained truly, really and substantially the body and blood together with the soul and divinity of our Lord Jesus Christ, and consequently the whole Christ, but shall say that he is in it only as in a sign, or figure or force — anathema sit.[14]

It is Roman Catholic dogma that in the mass the Lord Jesus Christ is sacrificed, i.e. offered to God by way of death. Canons 2 and 3 of Session XXII of Trent state:

> If anyone shall say that the sacrifice of the Mass is only one of praise and thanksgiving; or that it is a mere commemoration of the sacrifice consummated on the cross . . . anathema sit.[15]

Here, two ideas of sacrifice are explicitly stated and just as explicitly repudiated. They are that the sacrifice of Christ in the eucharist is not one of praise, as the Church worships, nor one of recollection, as the Church remembers His death. The sacrificial element lies elsewhere. Where is it to be found? The following statement makes this clear:

> And inasmuch as in this divine sacrifice which is celebrated in the Mass there is contained and immolated in an unbloody manner the same Christ who once offered himself in a bloody manner on the altar of the cross . . . For the victim is one and the same, the same now offering by the ministry of the priests who then offered himself on the cross, the manner of offering alone being different.[16]

This is an important statement, together with the sentences which follow it. These will be quoted later. For our present purpose, the statement makes clear that Christ is both contained in the mass and that He offers Himself by way of the mass. These two matters call for examination.

a) How is it possible that Christ is 'truly, really and substantially' contained in the mass?

The Roman Catholic answer to this question is found in the dogma of transubstantiation. Trent declares:

> It has . . . always been a firm belief in the Church of God, and this Holy Council now declares it anew, that by the consecration

of the bread and wine a change is brought about of the whole substance of the bread into the substance of the body of Christ our Lord, and of the whole substance of the wine into the substance of His blood. This change the holy Catholic Church properly and appropriately calls transubstantiation.[17]

Now this change in the substance of the bread and wine occurs when the words of consecration ('This is my body' and 'This is my blood') are uttered in all sincerity by a duly ordained priest. What is more, it occurs without any change taking place in the appearance of either the bread or the wine. Nevertheless, the change of substance, it is claimed, has occurred so that 'the true body and the true blood of the Lord, together with his soul and divinity, exist under the form of bread and the blood under the form of wine, by the power of the words.'[18] Furthermore, it is argued that, as Christ's divinity was truly united with His body and soul, His body exists under the form of wine and His blood under the form of bread.

Trent concludes: 'Wherefore it is very true that as much is contained under either form as under both.'[19]

It is in this way that the withholding of the cup from the laity is justified. The whole Christ is contained in the bread, that is to say, the host.

The seriousness, with which the reality of this change is both taught and believed, is indicated by the elevation of the host, by the way in which it is carried about in Corpus Christi processions and by its use in the service of benediction to bless the people. Trent declares:

> There is, therefore, no room for doubt that all the faithful of Christ may, in accordance with a custom always received in the Catholic Church, give to this most holy sacrament in veneration the worship of Latria, which is due to the true God . . . For we believe that in it the same God is present of whom the Eternal Father, when introducing him to the world, says 'And let all the angels of God *adore* him' (Hebrews 1:6); whom the Magi, falling down, adored (Matthew 2:11); who, finally, as the Scriptures testify, was adored by the Apostles in Galilee (Matthew 28:17).[20]

Worship in the Roman Catholic Church is distinguished between what is due to God alone (*Latria*), what may be given to the saints (*dulia*) and what is given to Mary (*hyperdulia*). We shall lay aside for a moment the belief that these are distinctions without any real difference and accept their importance for Roman Catholic theology. We must note the fact that the kind of worship to be given to the host is that which is reserved for God alone. This arises from the belief that Christ, the Son of God, *is* in the host.

b) How can Christ offer Himself to God by way of the mass?

It will perhaps have been appreciated already that the consecration of the elements which accomplishes their transubstantiation belongs to the ministry of the priests. Indeed, it belongs to them exclusively.

One of the reasons why Pius XII issued his encyclical *Mediator Dei* was in order to emphasize the particular character and power of the priesthood within the context of the growing role of the laity in the liturgy. Pius XII asserts: 'The fact that the faithful take part in the Eucharistic Sacrifice does not mean that they also possess the power of the priesthood.'[21] Priestly power is not delegated to the priest by the people. It is communicated to the priest by Christ whom he represents. As Pius XII teaches:

> The priest acts in the name of the people precisely and only because he represents the person of our Lord Jesus Christ, considered as Head of all the members and offering himself for them; . . . the priest, therefore, approaches the altar as Christ's minister, lower than Christ, but higher than the people . . . the people, on the other hand, because it in no way represents the person of the divine Redeemer and is not mediator between itself and God, can in no way possess the priestly right. All this is certain with the certainty of faith.[22]

Furthermore, this distinction between priest and people is maintained even in the context of their co-operative offering of the host.

> To avoid any mistake in this very important matter we must clearly define the exact meaning of the word 'offer'. The unbloody immolation by which, after the words of consecration have been pronounced, Christ is rendered present on the altar in the state of victim, is performed by the priest alone, and by the priest in so far as he acts in the name of Christ, not in so far as he represents the faithful. But precisely because the priest places the divine victim on the altar he presents it as an oblation to God the Father for the

63

glory of the blessed Trinity and for the benefit of the whole Church. Now, understood in this restricted sense, the oblation is in their own way shared by the faithful, and for two reasons: first because they offer the sacrifice *through* the priest, and secondly because, in a certain sense, they offer it *with* him.[23]

In spite of what the faithful are here said to be doing, and in spite of the confessed 'power of words', namely, 'This is my body' and 'This is my blood', it is only when these words are uttered by someone sacramentally ordained by a bishop (i.e. in apostolic succession to Christ Himself) that transubstantiation occurs and offering can take place. Though the words uttered are the Lord's own, it is the official status and distinctive sacramental character of the one uttering them which accomplishes what they allegedly proclaim. This makes the priest an *alter Christus* — 'a second/another Christ'. This does not mean that he is different from Christ, but rather that he is a continuation of the Christ in the Church. Behind this is the theology of the Church as an extension of the incarnate Christ and His ministry while He was on earth.

One final point in this examination of Roman Catholic teaching concerns the purpose for which Christ is offered to God in the mass. The Roman Catholic Church teaches that the mass is both propitiatory and petitionary, but primarily propitiatory. This can be seen in the following statements made by the Council of Trent:

> And inasmuch as in this divine sacrifice which is celebrated in the Mass there is contained and immolated in an unbloody manner the same Christ who once offered himself in a bloody manner on the altar of the cross, the Holy Council teaches that this is truly propitiatory and has this effect that if, contrite and penitent, with sincere heart and upright faith, with fear and reverence, we draw nigh to God we obtain mercy and find grace in seasonable aid (Hebrews 4:16). For, appeased by this sacrifice, the Lord grants the grace and gift of penitence, and pardons even the gravest crimes and sins. For the victim is one and the same, the same now offering by the ministry of priests who then offered himself on the cross, the manner of offering alone being different. The fruits of that bloody sacrifice, it is well understood, are received most abundantly through this unbloody one, so far is the latter from derogating in any way from the former. Wherefore, according to the tradition of the apostles, it is rightly offered not only for the

64

sins, punishments, satisfactions and other necessities of the faithful who are living, but also for those departed in Christ but not yet fully purified.[24]

This is obviously a very important statement and we shall consider it under three headings, namely scope, virtue and bearing. The last-mentioned of these will lead us to the heart of what we are seeking to consider, namely, the mass *and the cross*.

Scope

It would be hard to think of anything excluded from the alleged scope of the virtue of the mass. In its propitiatory aspect, it placates and appeases the justice of an angered God against a sinner. It deals with the stain and penalty of sins of the living and the departed. In its petitionary aspect, it intercedes for all kinds of needs. The mass offered in the Falklands crisis is an example of its petitionary use.

Virtue

The Latin phrase *ex opere operato* which means 'by virtue of the performance of the act' indicates that there is an efficacy inherent in the mass as in the other sacraments of the Roman Catholic Church. Trent declares: 'If anyone shall say that the sacraments of the New Law do not contain the grace which they signify . . . If anyone shall say that by the sacraments of the New Law grace is not conferred ex opere operato, let him be anathema.'[25] By the use of the term 'New Law' a contrast with Jewish law is intended. Yet the efficacy inherent in the mass is maintained in spite of a simultaneous insistence upon the worthy attitude or faith of the communicant. That faith is described as follows: 'If anyone shall say that they (the sacraments) do not confer that grace (which they signify) on those who place no obstacles in its way . . . let him be accursed.'[26]

Clearly, the grace is in the sacrament, but faith is reduced to passivity.

Bearing

There is, therefore, a relation between the mass and the cross. On the other hand, so much is attributed to the mass that a consequent diminishing of the virtue of the cross seems inevitable. This Trent denies. It sees no difficulty; it asserts and glories in the relationship. This is evident from the statement quoted earlier on (see p.62): 'The fruits of that bloody sacrifice . . . are received most abundantly through this unbloody one, so far is the latter from derogating in any way from the former.' Trent further declares: 'If anyone shall say that by the sacrifice of the Mass a blasphemy is cast upon the most holy sacrifice of Christ consummated on the cross, or that the former derogates from the latter — let him be anathema.'[27]

We must now proceed to examine the relationship between the cross and the mass a little more precisely. It is possible that the term 'repeated' (or some variant of it) might come to mind as descriptive of this interrelationship. If that were the case, it would be thought (and possibly taught) that Roman Catholic teaching regarded the mass as a repetition of Christ's death on the cross. This would be terminologically inaccurate, and it would be strongly opposed by Roman Catholics. Unless Protestants are therefore familiar with the phrasing of Roman Catholic teaching on this matter, their apologetic activity will be ineffective and perhaps invalid.

The term used by Trent and favoured certainly by contemporary Roman Catholic theologians is not the term 'repeated'. Indeed, the term *once* is often used by them of the death of the Lord Jesus Christ, because as a historical event and a personal experience it is unrepeatable. It cannot happen all over again as if it had never happened before. The priest is therefore not to be thought of as 're-crucifying' Christ or putting Him to death all over again. The favoured term is 'represented', and this is used in the context of an accomplished death. Trent says:

> Though he was by his death about to offer himself once upon the altar of the cross to God the Father that he might there accomplish an eternal redemption, nevertheless, so that his priesthood might not come to an end with his death, at the last supper . . . so that he might leave to his beloved spouse the Church a visible sacrifice, such as the nature of man requires, whereby that bloody sacrifice *once to be accomplished* on the cross might be *represented*, the memory thereof remain even to the end of the world, and its salutary effects *applied* to the remission of those sins which we daily commit . . . [he] offered up to God the Father his own body and blood under the form of bread and wine and under the forms of those same things gave to the Apostles, whom he then made priests of the New Testament, commanding them and their successors in the priesthood by these

words to do likewise 'Do this in remembrance of me' [italics mine].[28]

This is a complete statement on the mass. What concerns us now is the fact that accomplishment and representation are mentioned in the same sentence. If words mean anything, there is a very fine but crucially important distinction here.

What is meant by 're-presentation'? That is how the word should be pronounced, because it does not mean that something is represented to us through its symbols, but rather that it is *made present all over again* in the midst of the Church. Christ is present as a sacrificial victim all over again in the mass and so offers Himself to God. Berkouwer aptly sums this up as follows: 'Christ's redemptive act becomes a new reality in the cult. His work is, so to speak, corporealized in the mass. Therein lies the essence of the doctrine of the mystery, that the divine redemptive act becomes a reality ever again.'[29] This is intimately related with the *application* of the benefits of Christ's death. There must be a sacramental re-presentation for the sacrifice on Calvary to be effective today, and this cannot happen apart from priestly activity in the context of the Church.

At this point we shall not begin an evaluation of Roman Catholic teaching in the light of the Scriptures and what they have to say above all about the cross of the Lord Jesus Christ. Such an evaluation is certainly required, and it is hoped that biblical passages and statements will have come to the reader's mind as we have proceeded. However, we are postponing such a critique and doing it for a particular reason. It is because some may believe that the present situation is different. Is not Roman Catholic doctrine changing and beginning to approximate to Protestant teaching? What of the statement produced by Roman Catholic and Anglican theologians in which a united way forward has been presented?

EUCHARISTIC DOCTRINE

Let us, therefore, turn to examine this statement. It claims to have bridged the divide between Roman Catholic and Anglican teaching on this subject. It is the ARCIC (i.e. Anglican-Roman Catholic International Commission) report entitled *Eucharistic Doctrine*, which was originally published in 1971. We must consider it together with its sequel entitled *Elucidation*. This later work was produced in 1979 in the light of comments and criticisms received about *Eucharistic Doctrine.*

The Anglican-Roman Catholic International Commission is a theological commission, which was inaugurated following the visit of Archbishop Ramsey to Rome in 1966. It received fresh impetus from the Common Declaration of Pope Paul VI and Archbishop Coggan made during the latter's visit to Rome in 1977. (This venture has of course continued as a result of the visit of John Paul II — see chapter three in this book.) The Commission isolated three areas of disagreement between the bodies which it represented. The three areas were the eucharist, the ministry, and authority, and the Commission concentrated attention on each of them in turn. The Commission's statements on each of these three subjects are now available in a paperback entitled *The Final Report*.[30] We shall consider the statement on the eucharist, though the other two statements are by no means irrelevant to this matter. Before we look at any of the details of this statement, it is important to notice three particular features of it.

1. The purpose of this statement

The aim of both this statement and those on ministry and authority is expressed in terms of 'the restoration of full organic unity' between the two Churches, that is, 'the restoration of complete communion in faith and *sacramental life*' (italics mine).[31] These italicized words indicate how crucial the eucharist is to this whole scheme and aim. Unless there is agreement on the eucharist, union is totally impossible. This statement is therefore very important to the entire ecumenical enterprise.

2. The claim made for this statement

Though an element of qualification is noticeable in what is said about this statement, its compilers still tell us enough to make it clear that in their unanimous judgment something of major significance has been achieved. They say that here is '"substantial agreement", which is consistent with "a variety of theological approaches within both our communions"'.[32]

Further, they say, 'We have reached agreement on essential points of eucharistic doctrine . . . though no attempt was made to present a fully comprehensive treatment of the subject, nothing essential has been omitted.'[33] Even more important, perhaps, is the following: 'Members of the Commission are united in their conviction "that if there are any remaining points of disagreement they can be resolved on the principles here established."'[34] Clearly, it is believed that something real and far-reaching has been achieved.

3. The method used in this statement

Both groups confess 'penitence for the past'. They are therefore resolved to avoid 'the emotive language of past polemics' and to pursue '*together* that restatement of doctrine which new times and conditions are . . . regularly calling for'. The members say, 'We have been concerned, not to evade the difficulties, but rather to avoid the controversial language in which they have often been discussed'.[35] They are 'convinced . . . that substantial agreement on these divisive issues is now possible'.[36]

From these quotations and observations it will be appreciated that this document calls for careful evaluation. It may be likened to an exercise in re-routing, in which the motorist is prevented from taking a particular road and required to take a different one. Applied theologically to the case under consideration, this means that an approach to this sacrament via sixteenth-century and seventeenth-century terms and concepts is forbidden, and that one via a different term and concept is commended.

This change of approach, it is claimed, is not only helpful for *the creation of a new future*, but it also *resolves the controversies of the past*. This is a big claim to make and it will be tested in what follows.

The kind of questions that need to be borne in mind as we proceed with this study are:

1. What happens to the sixteenth-century issues and terms? Are they evaded or examined, overlooked or resolved? What is the relation between ARCIC and the past?

2. If a new term and concept is proposed and used, has real agreement been reached? Have we been carried beyond the area of controversial teachings to some clear, solid and generally acceptable basis for agreement? How does the basis of this agreement appear in the light of the Bible?

69

ARCIC AND THE PAST

In the case of both religious communions represented on this Commission there are doctrinal formulations, issued in the sixteenth century, to which reference ought to be made and in the light of which this new document should be considered. For the Roman Catholic Church, extended reference has already been made to the Council of Trent and also to the Second Vatican Council. The Thirty-nine Articles of Religion of the Church of England have yet to be considered, and of these, Articles 25 to 31 relate to the Lord's Supper.[37] A detailed examination of these two sets of statements will reveal that behind them lay both an understanding of the other communion's position on this subject and a concern to refute it as precisely as possible.

Now how does this new statement appear in this light? Does it represent a real *rapprochement* between the positions upheld in the sixteenth century? Or is it a shift from them? And if so, is it by both parties or by one? What is the current situation?

Roman Catholicism

We have seen already that there is no alteration in the essence of Roman Catholic teaching about the mass in the four hundred years between Trent and Vatican II. The position taken in the former is explicitly endorsed in the latter. Is this consistency maintained in ARCIC or abandoned? The answer must be that it is upheld. There is *nothing in ARCIC which is incompatible with Trent or Vatican II*. Indeed there are places, where the ARCIC document, if it does not explicitly state traditional Roman Catholic teaching, nevertheless clearly makes allowances for it.

There are some factors which can be mentioned as evidence for a shift from Tridentine teaching, and so we shall deal with these first.

The non-use of the term 'mass'

This term appears only once in ARCIC, and then in association with other terms which have been used in the course of history to refer to what the Lord instituted in the upper room on the night of His betrayal. Though preference is given in ARCIC to another term, this does not represent any shift from traditional Roman Catholicism for the term *mass* is not the primary term used in Trent or Vatican II. There we find the very term used in ARCIC, namely the *eucharist*.

The insistence on the 'once-for-allness' of the death of the Lord Jesus Christ

ARCIC says:

> Christ's redeeming death and resurrection took place once and for all in history. Christ's death on the cross, the culmination of his whole life of obedience, was the one, perfect and sufficient sacrifice for the sins of the world. There can be no repetition of or addition to what was then accomplished once for all by Christ. Any attempt to express a nexus between the sacrifice of Christ and the eucharist must not obscure this fundamental fact of the Christian faith.[38]

In the absence of any knowledge of the actual contents of Trent or Vatican II on this subject, it could be concluded from this statement, particularly from its last two sentences, that here we have a definite, large and important shift from Tridentine teaching. But we have seen that Roman Catholic teaching does contain a repeated insistence on the 'once-for-allness' of Christ's death. What is more, Trent's description of the relationship between Calvary and the eucharist is not presented in terms of *repetition* or *addition*, so ARCIC is not correcting Trent when it denies the applicability of these terms. As we have seen, the relation between Calvary and the eucharist is construed in terms of *representation* and *application*, not repetition or addition.

The conclusion which is therefore to be drawn from these points is that ARCIC does not *negate* any constitutive aspect of the doctrine of Trent. But in addition to this, it can be maintained that it allows for it, or specifically endorses it, by means of some of its statements. Without any attempt to force the meaning of the text, these statements can be regarded as ones that countenance transubstantiation, inherent efficacy of the sacrament (*ex opere operato*), priestly activity, and continued offering — i.e. all the essentials of Roman Catholic teaching. The evidence for this is as follows:

> Communion with Christ in the eucharist presupposes his true presence, effectually signified by the bread and wine which, in this mystery, become his body and blood.[39]

> The elements are not mere signs; Christ's body and blood become

really present and are really given. But they are really present and given in order that, receiving them, believers may be united in communion with Christ the Lord.[40]

The question to be asked is: 'What do these words mean to the Roman Catholic who wrote them?' The answer must include transubstantiation and *ex opere operato* efficacy. This is partly recognized by a footnote in the ARCIC document, where we read:

The word transubstantiation is commonly used in the Roman Catholic Church to indicate that God acting in the eucharist effects a change in the inner reality of the elements. The term should be seen as affirming *the fact* of Christ's presence and of the mysterious and radical change which takes place. In contemporary Roman Catholic theology, it is not understood as explaining *how* the change takes place.[41]

Here the word 'change' is used and needs to be bracketed with the word 'become' in the other quotations. What this footnote *does* is to exclude any crassly materialistic or outmoded philosophical explanation of the *how* of transubstantiation. What it *does not do* is to deny all reality to transubstantiation. Indeed, by speaking of 'the mysterious and radical change which takes place', it countenances it.

It is here that we ought to refer to the section in the *Elucidation* entitled 'Christ's Presence in the Eucharist'. In that section a strenuous attempt is made to rid the terms 'become' and 'change' of any materialistic conception. The important statement on this is as follows:

Becoming does not here imply material change. Nor does the liturgical use of the word imply that the bread and wine become Christ's body and blood in such a way that in the eucharistic celebration his presence is limited to the consecrated elements. It does not imply that Christ becomes present in the eucharist in the same manner that he was present in his earthly life. It does not imply that this *becoming* follows the physical laws of this world.

At this point, we need to remember that the Roman Catholic doctrine of transubstantiation does not claim a material change in the elements, nor a confined localization of Christ's presence, much less a reincarnation! None of the denials made in the above quotation can therefore prove hurtful to Roman Catholic dogma, let alone fatal to it. Not a single one of these denials, nor all of them taken together, really answer the objection raised against these terms. What Roman Catholicism does claim is a mysterious and spiritual *transformation of these elements*. The last denial quoted above points in that direction. This is confirmed by the rest of the quotation, which continues as follows:

> What is here affirmed is a sacramental presence in which God uses realities of this world to convey the realities of the new creation: bread for this life becomes the bread of eternal life. Before the eucharistic prayer, to the question: 'What is that?', the believer answers: 'It is bread.' After the eucharistic prayer, to the same question he answers: 'It is truly the body of Christ, the Bread of Life.'[42]

This indicates a sacramental transformation which is no less real and has no less value than a physical one. However transubstantiation is explained, or purged of its more crass forms, the result is one and the same, namely the fusion of the physical with the spiritual. The charge, therefore, still sticks. *Becoming* means an actual transformation of bread and wine into body and blood.

We have seen already that in Roman Catholic teaching about the mass, a crucial place is given to the priest. ARCIC upholds this. In the statement on the Eucharist we read: 'It is the . . . Lord who . . . through his minister presides at that table.'[43] Furthermore, the minister utters 'the consecratory prayer'. Then:

> Through this prayer of thanksgiving, a word of faith addressed to the Father, the bread and wine become the body and blood of Christ by the action of the Holy Spirit, so that in communion we eat the flesh of Christ and drink his blood.[44]

One further quotation taken from the ARCIC statement on ministry and ordination completes the picture at this point. It reads as follows:

> Despite the fact that in the New Testament ministers are never called 'priests' . . ., Christians came to see the priestly role of Christ reflected in these ministers and used priestly terms in describing them. Because the eucharist is the memorial of the sacrifice of Christ, the action of the presiding minister in reciting again the words of Christ at the last supper and distributing to the assembly the holy gifts is seen to stand in a sacramental relation to what Christ himself did in offering his own sacrifice.[45]

73

From this, the necessity of a priest for the eucharistic process is perfectly deducible.

Finally, the charge that the ARCIC document contains the element of this continued offering of Christ in the eucharist is no fabrication, though the evidence for it may not be of the prima-facie kind. We have seen that Roman Catholic teaching conceives of the eucharist in terms of the application of the benefits of the cross, and not as either a repetition of it or an addition to it. Following its clear statement to this effect — namely, 'There can be no repetition of or addition to what was then accomplished once for all by Christ' — the ARCIC document goes on to say: 'Yet God has given the eucharist to his Church as a means through which the atoning work of Christ on the cross is proclaimed and *made effective* in the life of the Church' (italics mine).[46]

By itself, this italicized expression does not settle the question of whether ARCIC includes the element of a continued offering of Christ in the eucharist. It can at least be said, however, that this expression chimes in with Roman Catholic teaching. Furthermore, we may add to it the following: 'In the eucharistic prayer the church continues to make a perpetual memorial of Christ's death, and his members . . . enter into the movement of his self-offering.'[47]

The term 'memorial' is a very important one in the entire approach to the eucharist employed by this document, and we shall consider its use and significance later. Yet it is the final part of this quotation which is important just now, that is, 'the movement of his self-offering'. What does this mean? It means that in the eucharist, Christ continues to offer Himself to the Father in the action of the Church, which offers itself along with Him in consecration and gratitude. Basic to this view is the belief that though Christ's sacrifice on the Cross took place in time, it cannot be limited to time — a view not confined to Roman Catholic writers.[48] These five or six words — 'the movement of his self-offering' — say all that is necessary to teach a continued offering of Christ's body and blood in the eucharist.

From all this it can be said that ARCIC clearly allows for traditional Roman Catholic teaching and that the line from Trent to Vatican II can be extended to the present day. But what is now to be said about ARCIC and the Thirty-nine Articles?

Anglicanism

It must be remembered that a different status is accorded to the Thirty-nine Articles in Anglicanism from that which is given to the decrees of Trent within Roman Catholicism. This is because of a disagreement over where authority lies in the church. Nevertheless, the Articles remain a historic as well as a historical expression of Anglican doctrine, and they cannot yet be entirely confined to a museum of theological antiquities.

When we compare ARCIC with Articles 28-31, a very different picture emerges from that gained by our correlation of ARCIC and Trent. Whereas we have argued for a basic continuity between Trent and ARCIC, there is a basic discontinuity and even disagreement between the Articles and ARCIC. This is seen both in a general way and in particular details.

In general, what must not be overlooked is that the term of reference used in ARCIC, i.e. 'eucharist', is nowhere mentioned in these Articles. It has an honoured place in the formulations of Trent, but no place at all in the Articles. On this matter of a term of reference, ARCIC says: 'The eucharist has *become* the most universally accepted term' (italics mine).[49] While this may be true, it needs to be noted that this represents a change within Anglicanism since the sixteenth century. Is this a change to be welcomed or to be resisted?

In the Articles we find that every distinctive point of Roman Catholic doctrine (transubstantiation, *ex opere operato* efficacy, worship of the host) are all clearly stated and as clearly repudiated. The following statements prove this:

> Transubstantiation (or the change of the substance of Bread and Wine) in the Supper of the Lord, cannot be proved by holy Writ; but it is repugnant to the plain words of Scripture, overthroweth the nature of a Sacrament, and hath given occasion to many superstitions.
>
> The Body of Christ is given, taken, and eaten, in the Supper, only after an heavenly and spiritual manner. And the mean whereby the Body of Christ is received and eaten in the Supper is Faith.
>
> The Sacrament of the Lord's Supper was not by Christ's ordinance reserved, carried about, lifted up, or worshipped.
>
> The sacrifices of Masses, in the which it was commonly said, that the Priest did offer Christ for the quick and the dead, to have

remission of pain or guilt, were blasphemous fables, and dangerous deceits.[50]

Given all this, the question which has to be faced is. 'On what basis can there be any *substantial* agreement between Anglican and Roman Catholic theologians on this matter?' The largest and most important element in the reply to this question lies in the doctrine of *eucharistic sacrifice*. This supplies the key to the understanding of the agreement presented and recommended in ARCIC.

Though the designation 'eucharistic sacrifice' is not used in ARCIC, but only the term 'eucharist', the *Elucidation* makes it perfectly clear that this is what underlies those references. In the discussion of remembrance and sacrifice in the *Elucidation*, the writers say:

> In the exposition of the Christian doctrine of redemption, the word *sacrifice* has been used in two intimately associated ways. In the New Testament, sacrificial language refers primarily to the historical events of Christ's saving work for us. The tradition of the Church, as evidenced for example in its liturgies, used similar language to designate in the eucharistic celebration the *anamnesis* (memorial) of this historical event. Therefore it is possible to say at the same time that there is only one unrepeatable sacrifice in the historical sense, but that the eucharist is a sacrifice in the sacramental sense, provided that it is clear that this is not a repetition of the historical sacrifice.

As a result, they continue:

> There is therefore one historical, unrepeatable sacrifice, offered once for all by Christ and accepted once for all by the Father.

But they also say:

> In the celebration of the memorial, Christ in the Holy Spirit unites his people with himself in a sacramental way so that the Church enters into the movement of his self-offering.[51]

This phrase, 'the movement of his self-offering' which is linked together with the concept of a sacramental union between Christ and the Church, forms the basis of the idea of eucharistic sacrifice. The question one must ask is how this squares with Article 31, part of which has been quoted. On this subject Bishop Gore wrote:

76

> On the subject of the Eucharistic sacrifice our Thirty-first Article only excludes any treatment of it which in any way suggests the insufficiency of the one offering of Christ . . . Beyond this our formulas are silent.[52]

In Gore's estimation, therefore, the door lay open for a legitimate discussion of eucharistic sacrifice subject to that one proviso which he had stated. To be more exact, the door had already been open for some fifty years. The Tractarians, the men of the Oxford Movement, had been arguing for this since the 1830s. In 1958, Dr Michael Ramsey, who was then Archbishop of York, had said in his address at the centenary service of the Eucharistic Congress:

> The Tractarians recovered the doctrine . . . that in the Eucharist the sacrifice is that of Christ Himself. Having nothing of our own to offer, trusting only in Christ's one offering of Himself, it is that which we re-present to the Father as ourselves members of Christ's body, accepted only in Him.[53]

1958 was an important year for Anglicanism as far as the doctrine and use of the term 'eucharistic sacrifice' was concerned. It was presented at the Lambeth Conference that year and urged as a means by which the various traditions within Anglicanism could be blended. The Oxford Conference of Evangelical Churchmen devoted its 1961 Conference to this theme. Dr J.I. Packer declared: 'It represents a line of thought which individual theologians have canvassed for more than a generation, but which has never before received any sort of official sanction.'[54]

We need to turn Bishop Gore's expression into a question and ask whether the doctrine of eucharistic sacrifice does *in any way* suggest the insufficiency of the one offering of Christ. If it does, then it is liable to the same serious charge as that brought against the mass, namely, that like human wisdom and eloquence, it makes the cross of Christ 'of none effect' (1 Cor. 1:17). This is the subject which we must now consider.

What, then, is the doctrine of eucharistic sacrifice? One must not think of it merely in terms of the meaning of the word 'eucharist' (i.e. thanksgiving). Such eucharistic activity is an acceptable act of worship, through which the Church expresses its gratitude to the Father for His gift of salvation in Christ. This is chiefly what the author of Hebrews had in view in chapter 13, verse 15, of his letter. Eucharistic sacrifice rather considers the thanksgiving of the church in relation to two other doctrines: the timeless aspect of Christ's sacrifice on the cross and the union between Christ and the church. Further, the nature of a eucharistic sacrifice as defined above (a sacrifice of obedient thanksgiving) is regarded as determinative of the significance of the death of Christ. Because of all this co-mingling, it becomes possible to regard what Christ did on the cross as being made present, continued and made available in what the church does at the eucharist.

With regard to the first of these doctrines, the timeless aspect of Christ's sacrifice, the Lambeth statement has this to say:

> If the redeeming work of Christ is limited to the Cross as a past act in time, we can only be thought of as entering [i.e. in our Eucharistic worship] into this *wholly past action* either by remembering it or repeating it. This partly explains the quarrel at the time of the Reformation. *But we are now in a different climate of thought.*[55]

How is it different? It involves the following view of Christ's work:

> Though it [Christ's once-for-all sacrifice] cannot be repeated, it is not merely a past fact; it is not only an event in history, but the revelation of eternal truth.[56]

So the bishops say that the finished work of Christ is consummated in the resurrection and ascension. But then the term 'finished' no longer means finished in the usual sense of the word, that is, a completed act which in this case would refer to an accomplishment that deals perfectly with sin. The reason why that cannot be the meaning here is because it is the *consummation* which continues to deal with sin. In his monograph *The Finished Work of Christ*, Rev. A.M. Stibbs quotes several authors who teach this, e.g. E.J. Bicknell, who wrote: 'So our Lord, by his presence within the veil, is now making atonement for us.'[57]

This is a doctrine which is repugnant to the Thirty-nine Articles and to Scripture. It has the effect of focusing attention in the eucharist no longer upon Christ's death on the cross, but upon His life in heaven.

Once the idea is accepted that Christ is continuing His work of atonement in heaven, the way is opened through the doctrine of

Christ's oneness with His church to incorporate what the church does on earth in the eucharist with what He is doing in heaven. This is what lies behind the statement in the ARCIC document that 'his members . . . enter into the movement of his self-offering'. As Christ's sacrifice for man was one of thanksgiving and obedience to the Father in relation to death, so the church's sacrifice in Him is of the same kind. As the church is one with Him, it is His sacrifice. In the Lambeth report, the bishops commend the words of Dr A.G. Hebert. They are as follows:

> The Eucharistic Sacrifice, that storm-centre of controversy, is finding in our day a truly evangelical expression from the 'catholic' side, when it is insisted that the sacrificial action is not any sort of re-immolation of Christ, not a sacrifice additional to His one Sacrifice, but a participation in it. The true celebrant is Christ the High Priest and the Christian people all assembled as members of His Body to represent before God His Sacrifice, and to be themselves offered up in Sacrifice through their union with Him.[58]

It is this world of thought which lies behind the idea of *memorial*. The words 'Do this in remembrance of me' have been construed as being equivalent to 'Offer this as a memorial of me'. Is this what ARCIC presents? The relevant statement on which a judgment about this must be based is the following:

> The notion of memorial as understood in the passover celebration at the time of Christ — i.e. the making effective in the present of an event in the past — has opened the way to a clearer understanding of the relationship between Christ's sacrifice and the eucharist. The eucharistic memorial is no mere calling to mind of a past event or of its significance, but the Church's effectual proclamation of God's mighty acts. Christ instituted the eucharist as a memorial of the totality of God's reconciling action in him. In the eucharistic prayer, the Church continues to make a perpetual memorial of Christ's death, and his members . . . enter into the movement of his self-offering.[59]

The *Elucidation* does not add anything material to this statement. Now, it must be admitted that nowhere in ARCIC is the expression 'Offer this as a memorial' found. Yet, that is the teaching which it presents. The memorial is something which the church makes, though Christ instituted it. In the making of this memorial, more is done than the recalling of a *past event* or of *its significance.* A proclamation takes place which is *effectual.* This means that by sacramental action the reality is made present and the church becomes caught up in the *movement of Christ's self-offering.* To whom did He offer Himself? It was to the Father. As He is really present in the church, He does the same along with it.

This idea of memorial is not in keeping with Old Testament teaching. The emphasis there is upon a reminder to men rather than to God. C.F.D. Moule, Lady Margaret Professor of Divinity at the University of Cambridge, has declared:

> For myself I remain wholly unconvinced by the attempts to make the anamnesis (*this do in remembrance of me*) mean that God is here reminded of what Christ has wrought, i.e. as though Christ's words meant 'Do this to remind God of me'.[60]

In the article from which this quotation is taken, Professor Moule refers to the careful linguistic and exegetical work of Mr Douglas Jones, who argues that the liturgical, Godward meaning of remembrance is not inherent in it. Mr Jones also adds the following:

> With some relief one feels freed of an interpretation which, if regarded as the primary and exhaustive meaning of our Lord's command, seems to come near to transforming the community of disciples, and therefore the Church, into some sort of mediator between God and his Christ, presenting to the divine memory at every Eucharist the story of his obedience and sacrifice that God may remember him and so effect his vindication at the last day.[61]

We are now in a position to reflect on both the mass and the eucharist as they have been described. While there are not unimportant differences between them, there are striking similarities. We have seen in connection with both that there is an insistence on the *once-for-allness* of Christ's sacrifice on the cross, not only as an event in history, but also, and more importantly, as an event in salvation. Yet, we have also noted that neither regards Christ's sacrifice as wholly past with its effects continuing into the present (which was the position espoused at the Reformation), but rather *as needing to continue* so that its effects might be bestowed and enjoyed.

Further, while there is agreement about the continuing nature of Christ's sacrifice, there is a difference about the kind of necessity which gives rise to it and the means by which it is made present. In Roman Catholic teaching, this necessity arises out of sins committed by the faithful subsequent to baptism. While some Anglicans agree with this, others see this necessity as arising from the impossibility of confining Christ's sacrifice to a single moment of time. (But here the lines of demarcation begin to be blurred and some Anglicans would take neither of these positions.) With regard to the means by which Christ's sacrifice is made present in the church, Roman Catholic teaching emphasizes the priest and transubstantiation. Though some Anglicans also believe this, others think in terms of the eternal high priesthood of the Lord and the activity of the Holy Spirit in the church. However, both emphasize the re-presentation and continuance of Christ's sacrifice in the eucharist.

These differences cannot be overlooked or minimized, nor can the two positions be presented as though they were in reality identical. Yet the oneness between them in terms of the doctrine of the continuance of Christ's sacrifice in the eucharist offered to God does enable them to be evaluated together in the light of Scripture. Dr J.I. Packer rightly says of eucharistic sacrifice: 'This may not be *exactly* a return to the Mass, but it is *certainly* a reversal of the Reformation' (italics mine).[62] Indeed, the unanimous teaching of the Reformation on this point was, as we shall now try to show, nothing but the teaching of the New Testament.

CHRIST'S SELF-OFFERING: THE TEACHING OF THE NEW TESTAMENT

In spite of references being made by both sides to Hebrews 9, there are certain statements in that chapter which are fatal to the idea of any continuance of Christ's self-offering for sin. These are found in verses 24-26 which are here quoted in full:

> For Christ has entered, not into a sanctuary made with hands, a copy of the true one, but into heaven itself, now to appear in the presence of God on our behalf.

> Nor was it to offer himself repeatedly, as the high priest enters the Holy Place yearly with blood not his own; for then he would have had to suffer repeatedly since the foundation of the world. But as it is, he has appeared once for all at the end of the age to put away sin by the sacrifice of himself. (RSV)

In these verses we are told what Christ is *not* doing in heaven. This is explained in terms of what the Jewish high priests were doing on earth, namely, offering a sacrifice to God. Christ did not enter heaven in order to do that. He had already done that when He appeared *at the end of the age*, i.e. the end of the period of predicted preparation. He entered heaven to intercede for sinners. This means that there is an aspect of our Lord's work as the high priest of His people which *has been terminated*. It is His putting away of sin by the sacrifice of Himself — the basis on which He exercises a continuing priestly ministry in terms of intercession. This biblical distinction is completely obliterated by the Roman and Anglican doctrine of eucharistic sacrifice. .

Another truth which these verses teach is the impossibility of an offering for sin without suffering for sin. This decisively rules out the notion of an 'unbloody sacrifice which deals with sin' (Trent) that lies at the root of the mass and eucharistic sacrifice. In verse 25 the word 'offer' is used, but in verse 26 the word 'suffer' appears. This change from 'offer' to 'suffer' is not only striking, but significant. It declares that it is impossible to offer for sin without suffering for sin. To offer for sin means to take it away, and this cannot be achieved without sin's penalty being borne. This necessitates suffering, for sin's wages is death (Rom. 6:23). Calvin has written:

> Though they insist a hundred times that this sacrifice is bloodless, I will reply, that it depends not on the will of man to change the nature of sacrifice, for in this way the sacred and inviolable institution of God would fall.[63]

If Christ entered heaven to offer frequently, He would need to suffer frequently. The notion is expressed in this way to point out how ridiculous, and indeed how blasphemous, it is.

One further truth in Hebrews 9:24-26 is relevant. It arises from the perfection of Christ's offering for sin. He would have had to repeatedly offer and suffer *before* Calvary as well as after it, if He had not dealt with sin perfectly by His one act of self-giving in obedience to God and in accordance with God's penalty for sin. The mass is argued for on the basis of the continuing sins of the faithful. What of the sins of Old Testament believers? How can they be dealt with on this basis? There is only one consistent alternative to one Calvary, namely, many Calvaries, before and after the one that was there in space and time. But Christ could not die before He was born. If there is need for a repeated self-offering *after* the cross, there is the same need for frequent self-offering in death *before* it. But His once-for-all offering of Himself to the Father through the Eternal Spirit deals with past and future sins. Christ was born **once** to live on earth — **once** to die for sin — **once**.

In addition to these biblical arguments and theological objections against the continuance of Christ's self-offering in either the mass or eucharist, there is one further objection to be brought. It is a most important one. It is practical and personal. The mass and the eucharistic sacrifice divert the sinner's gaze from *Jesus Christ and Him crucified.* For the Roman Catholic, what his Church does in worship is also bound up with salvation.

In both, the church can take the place in the sinner's mind and heart that the Saviour *alone* ought to occupy. To the extent that this is done, the worshipping sinner cannot enjoy the assurance of 'sins forgiven, of hell subdued, and peace with heaven'. Indeed, he or she may never know the saving effect of the death of Christ. But where the Saviour alone, as distinct from the church, and His death alone, as distinct from anything the church can do, are presented and regarded, proclaimed and believed in, the sinner's soul is filled with the assurance of eternal life.

3
Justification by Faith Alone

In the previous chapter we referred to the origin and purpose of the Anglican-Roman Catholic International Commission (see p.66f). With the publication of its findings on the subjects of authority, eucharist and ministry, it had fulfilled its brief. It was given a new lease of life, however, by Pope John Paul II and Archbishop Runcie in 1982. They assigned it the task of examining the vexatious but important subject of justification by faith. Because of the great importance of this doctrine to evangelicals in the Anglican Communion, the composition of the Commission was enlarged to include more men from their ranks. These were Rev. E.D. Cameron (Bishop of North Sydney), Rev. David Gitari (Bishop of Mount Kenya East) and Professor Oliver O'Donovan of Oxford University. They joined Rev. Julian Charley, an evangelical Anglican who had already served as a member of the original Commission (ARCIC 1).

SALVATION AND THE CHURCH

After three years of work the report of the enlarged Commission (ARCIC II) was published. Clifford Longley, the perceptive religious correspondent of *The Times* heralded it as a pact. The headline he used was: 'Churches settle salvation dispute. Reformation stumbling-block removed. Anglican-R.C. pact achieved'. In a later piece he wrote: 'The recent ARCIC agreed statement on salvation is rapidly transforming the atmosphere'.[1] In this chapter, however, we shall argue that ARCIC II has not faced the issue of justification by faith squarely, and that it has therefore failed to deal adequately with the subject.

PREFACE

The title of the report is somewhat surprising. *Salvation and the Church* is a strange way of summarizing a statement about justification by faith. It is, however, a reliable guide to the content of the statement and to the approach which members of the Commission adopted in their study of the subject. In the preface, the two co-chairmen explain the choice of the title as follows:

> The doctrine of justification . . . *can be properly treated only* within the wider context of the doctrine of salvation as a whole. This in turn has involved discussion of the role of the Church in Christ's saving work. Hence the title of our agreed statement [italics mine].[2]

The above italicized words beg a larger question — one which is related not only to the way in which justification is treated in this report, but also to the way in which it is treated in the New Testament. Those who have framed the report claim that justification can be properly treated only when it is connected with:

(a) all the other constituent elements of salvation
and (b) the Church.

This is tantamount to saying that justification cannot properly be treated as a subject in its own right, i.e. as a distinct theological doctrine. That is plainly ridiculous. Such a view denies the validity of much theological endeavour in the past, and it also undercuts the need for the same in the present. The Commission has not heeded the plea made in 1982 by Dr Alister McGrath of Wycliffe Hall, Oxford:

> May we ask that the current ecumenical discussions on justification pay attention to the question of what justification itself means, instead of concentrating on matters on which agreement can be expected as a matter of course: for example, in asserting the Christocentric or anti-Pelagian character of any 'ecumenical' doctrine of justification. Much work remains to be done; let us hope that it is done and is not overlooked for the sake of convenience.[3]

It is, of course, recognized that in the New Testament connections are made between justification, salvation and the church, and that scholars from the various disciplines of theological study should investigate them. It is not only Anglicans and Roman Catholics who perceive this; evangelical nonconformists do so too. The latter see justification as a major part of salvation, and the church as being composed of those who profess to have received the salvation which is in Christ by faith. But such a view would presumably not be acceptable to those who drew up this report because, in their eyes, it appears to demote the church. However, we need to note here the main point of general criticism which this chapter makes of the report. Although the New Testament does speak of justification in association with salvation and the church, in some passages it also deals with justification as if there were no other element in salvation, and as if there were no organism or organization such as the church. The answer of the apostle to one who asked 'What must I do to be saved?' mentioned neither sanctification nor the church. The answer was: 'Believe in the Lord Jesus' (Acts 16:30,31 NIV). Was this an *improper* way of dealing with justification? Surely not.

In addition to this evangelistic setting, there were times in the life of the New Testament churches when the doctrine of justification by faith needed to be presented in all its starkness and clarity. We can see this, for example, in Galatians and Romans. It is therefore not 'improper' to concentrate narrowly on justification in the ongoing life of the church. Indeed, it is essential to do so at times, because human beings have such a confidence in themselves that they will continue to invent fresh grounds for trusting anyone or anything apart from Christ *alone*.

In fact, could there have been a more natural and necessary place for a *concentrated* study of the doctrine than in this document? It is, after all, a statement on the very subject of justification by two communions, which have not only been divided over the matter but have also been studying it with a view to uniting again, if at all possible. Sadly, *that* kind of study is absent from this report. It does *not* present justification by faith in its biblical distinctness at all. The notes of this report are muffled, its lines are blurred and the issues are fudged. That is the case on both historical and biblical grounds. It is a most serious fault. Dr Alister McGrath declares that his evaluation of the report — especially those parts of it which he subjects to strong questioning — is justified by the 'need to ensure that we really are dealing with *genuine* agreement, rather than a diplomatic evasion of disagreement'.[4]

The excerpt from the report's preface, which has already been quoted, makes it clear that the methodology used for its production was chosen in the light of the ecumenical goal of the task, i.e. 'the restoration of full ecclesial communion'[5] between the two bodies. The preface also declares that 'unless there is assurance of agreement on this issue, there can be no full doctrinal agreement between our two Churches'.[6] At the end of the report we read: 'We are agreed that this is not an area where any remaining differences of theological interpretation or ecclesiological emphasis, either within or between our Communions, can justify our continuing separation.'[7]

The report says that the growth of mutual understanding between those involved in the Ecumenical Movement had contributed in a positive way to its production. It singles out for particular mention the report of the Lutheran and Roman Catholic Consultation. The latter is a detailed piece of theological study. It was published together with material based on discussions of certain sections of the New Testament.[8] The approach of *Salvation and the Church* is therefore ecumenical. It is of the kind which followed the Third World Faith and Order Conference at Lund in 1952.[9]

THE REPORT ITSELF

We must now examine the main body of the ARCIC II report. It is divided into paragraphs. Paragraph 1 is a general theological statement which aims to avoid all controversial issues. Paragraphs 2-8 are examples of ecumenical historiography and paragraphs 9-31 of ecumenical theology. It is evident from these paragraphs that the two sides have sought to iron out their differences with respect to the doctrine of justification by faith.

Justification by faith: historical treatment

In the historical treatment of the subject, two things have happened. First, agreement between the disputants at the Reformation has been maximized, while disagreements have been minimized. Secondly, the report describes even the disagreements as largely the result of misunderstandings, suspicions and fears. After making due allowance for the existence of misunderstandings at the time, Dr McGrath declares:

'Alongside this real, if obscured, agreement was genuine disagreement, where each side understood well what the other was saying, and took exception to it.'[10]

He specifies two issues which comprise the real heart of the Reformation controversy, namely, the formal cause of justification and the doctrine of assurance. He declares that the document is 'reluctant to address the real disagreements which classical Anglican theologians perceived to exist between themselves and Rome.'[11]

One may justly claim that such a method of treatment reduces the greatest upheaval in the western world to an unnecessary dispute about words. Rev. Julian Charley has sought to rebut this charge by pointing out that the report does not attribute the conflict to these misunderstandings. He writes: 'The Commission was certainly not playing down the profound disagreements that surfaced at the time.'[12]

If these disagreements *had* been stated in the report (they were in the Lutheran-Roman Catholic statement), it would have been much easier to accept that no attempt had been made to avoid them. In the absence of such material, the claim that ARCIC II does not consider anything *real* to have been at stake in the Reformation conflict should be allowed to stand.

In fact, the report attempts to open up a divide between the continental reformers and the Church of England on this subject. It declares that the former (and not the latter) were the strong critics of justification as defined by the Council of Trent. As the Articles of the Church of England had not been drawn up at the time of Trent, its definitions and anathemas were not to be regarded as directed against that body. This argument is rather lame to say the least. Dr Roger Beckwith comments on this historical reconstruction as follows: 'It would be difficult to think of one Anglican theologian (certainly none of those named in the Report) who could properly be described as "sympathetic" to Trent's decree on justification.'[13]

Dr Alister McGrath shows how Trent had no brief to deal with the situation in England, and no call to address the situation in Europe either except in conjunction with the views of Luther. However, Luther's influence in England after 1520 was considerable, because the ground had already been prepared by other exponents of justification. McGrath calls Tyndale a 'Luther clone'[14] and declares:

Trent may not have aimed its barbs at the Church of England —
but, like an allied state which finds itself drawn into a conflict not
of its own making, the Church of England moved expeditiously to
place itself in the Tridentine firing line. The Church of England
made the doctrine of justification an issue of division with Rome
. . . and . . . its theologians had no hesitation in identifying certain aspects of the doctrine as the chief points of their polemic
against the Roman Catholic Church.[15]

From all this it ought to be clear that the historical section
leaves much to be desired and that no Anglican evangelical
ought to be content with it. In the symposium on ARCIC II
published by *Evangel*, Dr David Wright shows how superficial
and partial the treatment is.[16]

Justification by faith: theological interpretation

We will now concentrate on what ARCIC II says about justification from a biblical and theological point of view. The report
acknowledges the help gained from 'the renewal of biblical
scholarship' and 'the development of theological studies' in its
formulation. We must therefore remember the re-emergence of
biblical scholarship in the Roman Catholic Church which had
been encouraged by Vatican II. We must also bear in mind the
various features of twentieth-century theological study which lie
behind this report and which have helped to make it what it is. A
common feature of all these theologies, however diverse they
may be, is the absence of a proper doctrine of Scripture as God's
written Word.[17] The adjective *holy* is not used of Scripture in
this report. That may be deliberate.

This weakness can be seen in the way in which the report uses
words like 'terms', 'concept' and 'idea' to describe what Scripture says.[18] Now, of course, this is what biblical statements are.
But they are more than that! They are divine truths and infallible
doctrines. A failure to emphasize this fact leaves the way wide
open for people to read the language of Scripture as if it were
but a human attempt at description rather than a divine means
of revelation. It is one thing to acknowledge the use of terms and
their meaning, but quite another to adhere to that meaning in
doctrinal formulation. Paragraph 18, for example, speaks of the
need for these 'ideas' and 'images' to be *interpreted*.[19]

In his Latimer Study, Dr McGrath draws attention to this. He
points to the difficulty encountered in bringing New Testament

evidence to bear on ecclesiological matters and notes the influence which tradition exerts upon the discussion of the subject. From this he deduces the fact that to non-evangelical Anglicans and Roman Catholics, New Testament evidence and doctrine are not the same thing. He writes: '"Doctrine" is not identical, nor even necessarily related to, the New Testament witness, which may be marginalized in relation to other sources of alleged authority.'[20]

This is sadly true nowadays and it is a most serious situation. It is, however, not only destructive of the doctrine of justification by faith, but is now destroying all the constituent doctrines of authentic Christianity. Given that fact, Dr McGrath's next statement is disappointing at least. He writes: 'The present writer has no intention of criticizing such a position: it is simply necessary to note that it exists.'[21] We hope that the explanation of this statement is that Dr McGrath considered the subject he was raising to be outside the limit of his paper.

We have seen that modern theology is characterized not only by a denial of the verbal inspiration and complete infallibility of Scripture, but also by a recognition of Tradition both alongside of it and above it.[22] Tradition is not specifically mentioned in this report. Nevertheless, its presence is evident from the decisive influence which it has exercised upon it. We read, for example:

> The theologians of the Reformation tended to follow the predominant usage of the New Testament in which the verb *dikaioun* usually means 'to pronounce righteous'. The Catholic theologians, and notably the Council of Trent, tended to follow the usage of patristic and medieval Latin writers, for whom *iustificare* (the traditional translation of *dikaioun*) signified 'to make righteous'.[23]

In response to this statement Dr Beckwith points out:

> The report is much too kind to Trent, saying that it follows 'the usage of patristic and medieval Latin writers'. Actually, this non-biblical use of the term was by no means universal among the Latin Fathers, or even among the Latin writers of the Middle Ages.[24]

However, after making the point about the two views of the meaning of *dikaioun* and declaring the forensic translation to be the biblical one, the report does not adopt it as its own. It permits the other translation to survive. It does this in spite of the fact that Old and New Testament linguistic and exegetical studies (Küng included, though he tries to have it both ways) favour the forensic rendering.[25] To fail to outlaw the meaning 'to make righteous', as this report does, is to allow Tradition a theological status which is not only both independent of Scripture and contradictory to it, but also superior to it.

It is precisely at this point that the basic theological error, which bedevils the whole statement, occurs. Permitting *iustificare* as a rendering of *dikaioun* opens up the way for the Roman Catholic confusion between justification and sanctification to enter into the document and thus to vitiate it.

We shall now focus our attention upon this merging of justification and sanctification by examining what the report has to say first of all about justification in relation to faith and good works, and then what it says about justification in relation to salvation and sanctification.

1. Justification in relation to faith and good works

The bearing of justification on faith and its bearing on works are treated separately in the report. Paragraphs 9-11 deal with faith and 19-24 with good works. Between these two sections the report considers justification in relation to other aspects of salvation, particularly sanctification.

On the matter of justification and faith, the report contains many unexceptionable statements including, for example, the following:

> The human response to God's initiative is itself a gift of grace, and is at the same time a truly human, personal response . . . Salvation is the gift of grace; it is by faith that it is appropriated . . . Our response to this gift must come from our whole being. Faith, therefore, not only includes an assent to the truth of the Gospel, but also involves commitment of our will to God in repentance and obedience to his call.[26]

Yet in spite of these assertions about the role of faith and grace in salvation, there is a glaring omission here. Given that it is by faith that salvation is received, what about the New Testament's unambiguous and categorical denial that works have *anything* to do with its reception? While in paragraphs 9-11 reference is made to New Testament texts, Romans 4:4-5 and Ephesians 2:8-9 are conspicuous by their absence. (The appearance of the latter in paragraph 19 is in another context, as we shall show.) Romans 4:5 declares: 'And to one who does not work but trusts him who justifies the ungodly, his faith is reckoned as righteousness' (RSV). Ephesians 2:8-9 affirms: 'For by grace you have been saved through faith; and this is not of your own doing, it is the gift of God — not because of works, lest any man should boast' (RSV).

These statements refer to justification (the narrower term) and salvation (the larger term) as being synonymous. They separate them from works (i.e. effort, merit, desert) in a total and unqualified manner. Salvation is given fully, freely and finally.

Justification (or salvation) is neither a consequence of works done, nor is it contingent on works being done, nor yet conditional on works to be done. It is the ungodly who are justified. It is the spiritually dead who are quickened into eternal life. The only reason why faith is required is that it alone harmonizes with God's way of salvation. We must renounce our works to trust in that way of salvation. In this section of the report, any positive words which are said about faith are spoiled by the report's failure to speak in negative terms about works.

Indeed, the *positive* way in which works are mentioned in this very section entitled 'Salvation and Faith' makes this failure even more serious. Although it omits the declaration that salvation is 'not of works', the report speaks of the necessity of works in connection with salvation. After referring to James 2:20, which states that 'faith without works is dead', the report continues:

> Living faith is inseparable from love, issues in good works and grows deeper in the course of a life of holiness. Christian assurance does not in any way remove from Christians the responsibility of working out this salvation with fear and trembling (Phil. 2:12-13) . . . The New Testament contains warnings against presumption (e.g. Col. 1:22ff, Heb. 10:36ff).[27]

The New Testament does indeed teach that good works are the necessary fruit of Christian love and of a holy life. What must be noted, however, is that good works are presented in the New Testament as *an indication (or test) of the genuineness of faith*. They are not joined with faith as the means by which that righteousness is received and the basis on which God justifies. The necessity of good works is not a doctrine which is in any way hurtful, let alone fatal, to the doctrine of justification by faith

93

alone. In the New Testament, a strong insistence on good works as a consequence of faith lies side by side with an equally strong insistence on justification/salvation by faith *without* good works. Why do they not lie side by side in this report? The fact that they do not shows that the report does not teach justification by faith alone.

An objection might well be laid against this claim on the basis of the following statement from paragraph 19, which does contain a reference to Ephesians 2:8ff and to the phrase 'not because of works':

> While we are not saved *because of* works, we are created in Christ *for* good works (Eph. 2:8ff) 'Not because of works': nothing even of our best achievement or good will can give us any claim to God's gift of renewed humanity [italics original].[28]

In reply to such an objection it must be pointed out that this sentence does not refer to justification but to salvation, and to salvation in the sense in which the report construes it, namely, as something which includes more than justification. Therefore, to be told that we are not saved because of works is *not* the same as being told that we are not justified by works, particularly since good works are not unconnected with other aspects of salvation, such as sanctification. If the subject of the above-quoted sentence were justification, then the objection would negate our claim. As justification is not the subject, our claim can still stand that in this report justification is *not* by faith without works.

Indeed, that claim is strengthened by the first sentence of paragraph 19 which declares that 'justification and sanctification are aspects of the same divine act'.[29] We shall return to this statement again, but let us for the moment note that justification-sanctification is equivalent to 'renewed humanity'[30] and 'freedom in Christ'.[31] This necessarily includes works, so the theological gap between justification and sanctification is further closed as the quotation from St Augustine makes clear: 'The God who made you without you, without you does not make you just'.[32] While that is true of sanctification as understood in this report, it is not true of justification.

One further matter must be mentioned in connection with justification and faith. It concerns the object of faith, or to put it in another way, the ground of justification. Here again, the report speaks acceptably when it uses general terms such as

'Christ', 'the act of God through Christ', 'the mercy and grace of God' and 'the Gospel'. The New Testament speaks in this way too; but it also speaks more narrowly and more precisely on this matter.

The fact is that it is not enough to speak of Christ's death as the object of faith. It is the *character* of His death which is the object of faith. Time and again the New Testament refers to 'his blood'. Blood denotes sacrifice, and sacrifice means that a penalty for sin is inflicted by God and that propitiation is effected. When disobedient sinners break God's law, they expose themselves to His wrath which will be poured out upon them. The report leaves ever so much to be desired in this particular area. We are not, however, surprised at the omission. While the report uses the terms 'atoning' and 'sacrifice', it does not connect Christ's death with God's wrath against sin. Thus the Godward dimension — the *vital* dimension — of His death is passed over. Indeed, the report contains an expression which seems to deny this whole aspect. It is found in paragraph 13, where we read: 'The language of expiation or propitiation . . . drawn from the context of sacrifice, denotes the putting away of sin and the re-establishment of right relationship with God.'[33]

This means that expiation and propitiation are regarded or treated as synonyms. Strictly speaking, they are not. A *thing* may be *expiated* — in this context, sin is dealt with and removed. However, only a *person* can be *propitiated*, because to propitiate means 'to placate or appease anger'. That element is completely missing from this report because the reality of the wrath of God is denied.

This is not unimportant because the object of faith is the ground of justification. What is to be trusted for righteousness is the basis on which God justifies the ungodly. This is the righteousness of Christ in His death. Dr McGrath regards this together with the related question of assurance of salvation as 'the real focus of the Reformation controversies'.[34] It is the first of these which is of primary importance and which concerns us now. Luther maintained that the righteousness which is the basis of justification is Christ's righteousness and not the sinner's. Trent rejected this explicitly and deliberately. It asserted that while righteousness is provided by God, it was also located within the believer. However, *Salvation and the Church* does not face up to this pointed disagreement, which the men of the sixteenth century perceived and debated. Instead, the report either fudges the issue or denies its existence. It affirms: 'The righteousness of God our Saviour is not only declared in a judgement made by God in favour of sinners, but is also bestowed as a gift to make them righteous.'[35]

Dr McGrath has a piece of information on this subject which is very significant. It appears in his book *ARCIC II and Justification*. It follows the section where he describes how Anglicans in the sixteenth and early seventeenth centuries perceived that the nub of the issue against Rome was *the formal cause of justification*.[36] He then refers to Newman's *Lectures on Justification* which were first published in 1838. Between the first and third editions of that work, i.e. 1838 and 1874, Newman joined the Church of Rome. We shall let Dr McGrath make his own point:

> The sole alteration to the work which he [Newman] deemed necessary as a result of this conversion was the addition of a preface and an extensive appendix on the question of the formal cause of justification. It is at this point that Newman then perceived the crucial divergence between Anglicanism and Roman Catholicism.[37]

The basis, then, on which God justifies the guilty sinner who believes in Him, is what Luther has called 'the alien righteousness' of Christ. Because God has justly punished sin in the death of Christ, He can declare to be just all who trust in Christ. It is Christ's death as a vicarious and propitiatory sacrifice which is vital. Without it justification would be the height of injustice. God made His Son to be sin for His people by *imputing* their sins to Him and punishing Him for them, though He was personally without sin. By an identical act, but in reverse, God makes sinners righteous in His sight, by *imparting* Christ's righteousness to them — though they are sinners. They are, therefore, *simul iustus et peccator*.

Dr J.I. Packer has written in a definitive way about this as follows:

> Salvation in the Bible is by substitution and exchange: the imputing of men's sins to Christ, and the imputing of Christ's righteousness to sinners . . . The imputing of righteousness to sinners in justification, and the imputing of their sins to Christ on Calvary, thus belong together; and if, in the manner of so much modern Protestantism, the penal interpretation of the Cross is re-

jected, then there is no ground on which the imputing of righteousness can rest.[38]

It follows, of course, from this that the ground on which sinners are justified by God is also the ground on which they may be assured of eternal salvation.

The Commission's report on justification is open to serious criticism because of a *double confusion* and a practical *denial*. The *first confusion* arises from the failure to dissociate works from faith as the means by which justifying righteousness is received. The *second* goes deeper. It is that Christ's righteousness is mingled with the believer's righteousness as the ground or basis on which God justifies. The *denial* is the report's failure to recognize the nature of Christ's death as a vicarious and propitiatory sacrifice for sin.

2. Justification in relation to salvation in general and sanctification in particular

By treating justification in connection with other elements of salvation, *Salvation and the Church* is doing more than attempting to set it in a biblical context. It is protesting against the position of eminence which Luther, Calvin and others gave to justification by faith in the application or reception of salvation. It is also attempting to resituate it in twentieth-century ecclesiology. Dr Tim Bradshaw of Trinity College, Bristol, has rightly referred to ARCIC's 'recontextualizing methodology'.[39]

Luther's description of justification as 'the article of a standing or falling church' is well known. But he said more on its behalf than that. Dr McGrath quotes him as describing justification as 'instructor and chief, master, director and judge of all kinds of doctrines, which holds together and governs all church doctrine and establishes our conscience before God'.[40] In the same work McGrath not only argues for the primacy of justification, but shows how its constituent principles provide the parameters for a theology which is orthodox. By contrast, *Salvation and the Church* refuses to accord to it such a position and influence. Paragraph 18 declares:

> Thus the juridical aspect of justification, while expressing an important facet of the truth, is not the exclusive notion in the light of which all other biblical ideas and images of salvation must be interpreted.[41]

This effectively demotes justification from the place it occupied in the Reformers' interpretation of the Bible and in the theology which they derived from it. In doing this, the ARCIC II document is not breaking new ground.[42] The statement here goes further than this, however. It declares that no one idea, term, or concept is to fill the throne. (This is a consequence of the current emphasis on the human character and diversity of the Bible.) Paragraph 13 states: 'In order to describe salvation in all its fulness, the New Testament employs a wide variety of language. Some terms are of more fundamental importance than others: but there is no controlling term or concept; they complement one another.'[43]

If there is no controlling term or concept, then anything faintly resembling an *ordo salutis* — and the New Testament does speak in this way (cf. Romans 8:30) — becomes impossible. As a result, one's understanding of the application of salvation is confused, and one's interpretation of Scripture loses coherence and consistency. A further great loss follows from this. It concerns the point where a guilty sinner may be directed to find peace with God — the genesis of the Reformation. This is the 'wicket-gate admitting to the Christian life'. These words are not a quotation from any of the writings of John Bunyan, the nonconformist, though the expression is his. It comes from the unpublished commentary on Romans by an Anglo-Catholic, namely N.P. Williams — a former Lady Margaret Professor of Divinity at Oxford University. He regarded *dikaioun* in Romans as meaning 'to deem, declare or admit someone to be righteous, or in the right'. He wrote: 'It is thus the gateway to the Christian life, not a part or an event in that Christian life itself — a gateway which in the nature of things can only be passed once in a lifetime and once for all.'[44]

There can be no doubt that the report dislodges justification by faith from its prime position both hermeneutically and theologically. It deprives it of its clear and exclusive message to sinners (i.e. exclusive of other ways of salvation). It does this by bracketing justification with sanctification. At one stroke — and nothing could be more deadly — the sinner is directed, in part at least, to look to himself instead of away from himself and wholly to Christ. Paragraph 15 asserts: 'Justification and sanctification are two aspects of the same divine act.'[45]

It is 1 Corinthians 6:11 which the Agreed Statement immediately quotes in favour of conjoining sanctification and justification. By such a sanctification, the report means a 'sanctifying recreation . . . in grace . . . [a] transformation . . . being worked out in the course of our pilgrimage'.[46] Now that kind of sanctification is a *process* and not an act. On the other hand, the sanctification referred to in 1 Corinthians 6:11 is an *act* and not a process (the verb is in the same tense as the verb 'justified'): 'And such were some of you. But you were washed, you were sanctified, you were justified in the name of the Lord Jesus Christ and in the Spirit of our God.' (RSV)

Sanctification is spoken of in two ways in the New Testament. On the one hand, it is something which is completed at the beginning of the Christian life (cf. Acts 20:32; 26:18; 1 Cor. 1:2). On the other hand, it is a process which is only completed in heaven (cf. 1 Thess. 5:23; 1 Pet. 1:14-16). 1 Corinthians 6:11 comes into the first category but not the second.[47] On this point David Wright comments:

> On the basis of the former [i.e. completed sanctification], it may be entirely correct to affirm that 'Justification and sanctification are two aspects of the same divine act' (para.15), but this cannot apply to the latter, if only because a single 'divine act' is no longer in view . . . The damaging implications of this undifferentiated exposition become evident in the statement, 'By pronouncing us righteous, God also makes us righteous' (para. 15), where 'In addition to' is needed in place of 'By'.[48]

The result of this confusion is that our righteousness and our works become mingled with Christ's righteousness and faith. This is fatal for the biblical doctrine of justification.

The idea that God's word is a creative word is used by the Agreed Statement to support the merging of justification and sanctification. The report says:

> God's grace effects what he declares: his creative word imparts what it imputes. By pronouncing us righteous, God also makes us righteous. He imparts a righteousness which is his and becomes ours.[49]

This really is desperate. John Henry Newman himself used the creative word concept to link justification and sanctification in his attempt to construct a *via media* for himself between Anglicanism and Roman Catholicism.[50] Hans Küng repeats the idea in his work on justification.

It is of course true that God's word is powerful. It does effect what it declares, as is evident from the verse, '"Let there be light"; and there was light' (Gen. 1:3). But the all-important question is '*What* does God declare in justifying the ungodly?' He declares that they are justified — it is precisely that, and nothing more than that, which takes place. When, through Christ's righteousness, God declares a person just before His law (even though that person is unjust in himself), that is what the ungodly person becomes in God's sight. He does not become just in himself, but God now looks upon him as just. Forensic justification is not a legal fiction, but an actual fact in God's court. God's pronouncements cannot be regarded as effecting what they do *not* declare. With devastating logic Dr David Samuel has pointed out in his article in *The Times* that when God condemns, He does not make someone a sinner. Why then should He make someone righteous when He justifies them?[51]

The report says that there is no controlling term in formulating a doctrine of salvation. However, it is clear from the prominence given to sanctification over justification that the former has a better chance of being crowned — if ever there were such a crowning — than any other term. While we read that 'some terms are of more fundamental importance than others', it is evident that justification is not among them. Several words are listed in paragraph 13, but justification comes last of all. Even when a paragraph is given to the subject of justification (para. 18), it comes after one on sanctification. Furthermore, although paragraph 18 states: 'Instead of our own strivings to make ourselves acceptable to God, Christ's perfect righteousness is reckoned to our account', it continues as follows: 'God's declaration is *sometimes* expressed in the New Testament in the language of law, as a verdict of acquittal of the sinner' (italics mine).[52]

How else does God declare us to be righteous, we may ask? The spectre of inner righteousness lies behind this statement. We believe that James 2:14-20 speaks of the demonstration of faith to other human beings in such a way as to justify its existence over against an empty profession. Alternatively, it may signify the expression to God of a believer's faith by means of works to which God responds with pleasure. But such action is something which is subsequent to believing and does not imply working in order to be accepted initially into God's favour.

LUTHERAN-ROMAN CATHOLIC REPORT

Dr McGrath is more favourably disposed to the Lutheran-Roman Catholic report *Righteousness in the New Testament* than he is to ARCIC II. This is because the former acknowledges the existence of real disagreements and faces them, instead of attempting to marginalize or ignore them. In his view, a further point in its favour is that it does not try to make out that such disagreements are different ways of saying the same thing. He states that in the Lutheran-Roman Catholic report 'it is recognized that the concepts of justification by an external and intrinsic righteousness are totally different.'[53]

Yet, in spite of the fact that this report recognizes such great differences, Dr McGrath approves of its claim that 'neither excludes the other'. He repeats that the dialogue group hopes that the differences may be 'complementary rather than contradictory approaches to the doctrine.'[54]

It is true that the Lutheran-Roman Catholic dialogue eschews facile identification and confesses that difficulties did exist in the sixteenth century and that some still remain in the twentieth century. Yet, in spite of this, we fail to see any real difference between what they end up with and what ARCIC II presents. Both documents allow the two views of the nature of justifying righteousness to stand. That is the bottom line; the rest is playing with words. The Lutheran-Roman Catholic report declares:

> It must be emphasized that our common affirmation that it is God in Christ alone whom believers ultimately trust does not necessitate any one particular way of conceptualizing or picturing God's saving work. That work can be expressed in the imagery of God as judge who pronounces sinners innocent and righteous . . . and also in a transformist view which emphasizes the change wrought in sinners by infused grace.[55]

Of course, two different views can be compatible, but only if they do not contain an unavoidable mutual contradiction. But the two views of justifying righteousness do necessarily and unavoidably exclude each other. According to one view, God justifies sinners on the basis of Christ's righteousness *alone*; according to the other, God does *not* justify on the basis of Christ's righteousness *alone*. To say that both positions stress that God's saving work in Christ is the foundation of faith is to go no further than to affirm a Christological and anti-Pelagian doctrine which was not in dispute at the time of the Reformation. '*What must I do to be saved?*' is still the question which opens up an irremovable divide.

Conclusion

In this chapter we have argued that sanctification is given precedence over justification in *Salvation and the Church*. This is because the church is given theological precedence over the Bible and the gospel. The report quite explicitly assigns the church a role in salvation, and declares that salvation is received through baptism and incorporation into the Christian community. The relevant statement is: 'Salvation in all [its] aspects comes to each believer as he or she is incorporated into the believing community.'[56]

An editorial on this statement in *The Times* was much more perceptive than comments by Michael Baughen, Bishop of Chester, and by George Carey, former Principal of Trinity College, Bristol (now Bishop of Bath and Wells). Michael Baughen wrote: 'Most evangelicals in the Church of England will welcome [*Salvation and the Church*] with warmth . . . [it] contains excellent statements about justification'.[57] George Carey spoke of it as a 'major breakthrough . . . a clear and unambiguous statement on a doctrine that has separated Catholic and Protestant for over 400 years'.[58]

In contrast to these comments, *The Times* stated that 'the theology of justification is no longer a central issue in any church'. The editorial was significantly entitled 'Justification by Unity'.[59]

Dr J.I. Packer compares the doctrine of justification to Atlas. He says that 'it bears a world on its shoulders, the entire evangelical knowledge of saving grace'. He then adds:

> When justification falls, all true knowledge of the grace of God in human life falls with it, and then, as Luther said, the church itself falls.

But even this is not all. He concludes:

> A society like the Church of Rome, which is committed by its official creed to pervert the doctrine of justification, has sentenced itself to a distorted understanding of salvation at every point. Nor can these distortions ever be corrected till the Roman doctrine of justification is put right. And something similar happens when

Protestants let the thought of justification drop out of their minds: the true knowledge of salvation drops out with it, and cannot be restored till the truth of justification is back in its proper place. When Atlas falls, everything that rested on his shoulders comes crashing down too.[60]

4
Baptism, Eucharist and Ministry

Ecumenical writing is very much concerned with the church, and that is not altogether surprising. The subjects of baptism, eucharist and ministry certainly focus our attention very firmly upon it. We must stress, however, that evangelicals are not reluctant about taking up the study of ecclesiology. The criticisms expressed in the first and third chapters of this book against the treatment given to the church in the documents, which we were then examining, have not been directed against the church *per se*. Rather, our misgivings concern the prominence given to it in documents concerned with Scripture on the one hand and with justification by faith on the other. As there are subjects which can and should be discussed without the church being imported into the discussion, so there is a time and place for the church to receive attention. This is what we shall now proceed to do. This chapter will, however, only be the first part of our discussion of the church, because the next chapter will be devoted to the subject of mission — the role and task of the church in the world.

Baptism, Eucharist and Ministry[1] (which from now on we shall refer to as *BEM*) is the title of a document that was completed in 1982 by the Faith and Order Commission meeting at Lima in Peru. It is, therefore, also referred to as the 'Lima report'. Rev. Philip Morgan, the General Secretary of the British Council of Churches, describes it as 'the result of a process which began over 50 years ago with the First Faith and Order World Conference at Lausanne in 1927'.[2] This document has been strongly commended to all member churches of the WCC for study at all levels. In it, a response is sought to a number of questions. The most important of these (we judge) is the one which concerns *'the extent to which your church can recognise in this text **the faith of the Church through the ages**'*.[3] Though these last words do not appear in bold in the original, we highlight them here because they do beg a number of questions. We shall see that the expression 'the faith of the Church' is a very significant one in *BEM* and, indeed, in contemporary ecumenical ecclesiology.

We must first set this document within its historical context. We shall note the importance which ecumenists attach to it and the 'new' element which it contains. We shall then present an evangelical evaluation of the document in general and seek to substantiate that assessment by a review of its contents.

THE HISTORICAL SETTING

It is generally acknowledged that the production and publication of *BEM* was only possible because of the breakthrough achieved at Montreal. We have already referred to that Faith and Order Conference in the first chapter of this book. We noted that what was said at Montreal about Scripture and Tradition was bound to open up a freer approach to other theological issues on which there was disagreement in the WCC. The subjects of baptism, eucharist and ministry were also discussed at Montreal, and they have been on the agenda ever since. Study groups had been at work and in 1977 their reports eventually resulted in the establishment of a Steering Group to reduce the material to some shape. The Bangalore conference of 1978 received material from the conference held at Accra in 1974 and considered a statement which was finally settled at Lima in 1982. Nikos Nissiotis, the Moderator of the Faith and Order Commission, has written: 'This ecclesiological study is a part of the related effort to "Giving Account of the Hope that is in Us", which had been the previous Faith and Order theme concluded at its Bangalore Assembly.'[4]

In this whole process the contribution of Brother Max Thurian of the Taizé Community has been most influential. The details of these conferences are to be found in the preface to *BEM*.

The Faith and Order Commission has another project in hand and this is its major goal at present. It is entitled 'Towards a Common Expression of the Apostolic Faith Today'. *BEM* is part and parcel of that project, and responses to its own inquiries will be taken into account when the larger statement is drafted. *BEM* is also to be associated with another Faith and Order study entitled 'The Unity of the Church and the Renewal of Human Community'. Nissiotis has written:

> One should keep in mind this broad inter-relationship of study themes, when evaluating the text 'Baptism, Eucharist and Ministry'. All of them aim to make unity an instrument of the Church in its service to the world. It becomes immediately evident how important the BEM text is in this connection. There can be neither a common expression of the apostolic faith nor a concerted action of the churches in the world without agreement on these three basic ecclesial events which sum up church life and give it coherence and continuity.[5]

THE 'NEW' ELEMENT

The 'new' element which the document contains is bound up with the expression 'the faith of the Church through the ages'. The preface to the report claims that it exhibits 'a remarkable degree of agreement . . . That theologians of such widely different traditions should be able to speak so harmoniously about baptism, eucharist and ministry is unprecedented in the modern ecumenical movement.'[6] In a report to a Church of Scotland committee, Prof J.K.S. Reid has described the Lima gathering as 'the nearest thing to an ecumenical council since Nicaea II in 787'.[7]

Given that virtually all the major church traditions were represented, the expression 'the faith of the Church' is a most noticeable one. While all the church bodies were present at the Lima conference, there is only *one* faith of the church. Although Lima wants the churches to answer questions on this matter, one feels bound to ask, 'What is this *"faith of the Church"*?' The italics are mine, but the use of the capitalized form for the word 'Church' in the original is significant. Dr David Wright of New College, Edinburgh, has written on this point as follows. '"The faith of the Church through the ages" is an exceedingly elusive phenomenon . . . the divisions that have marked much of Christian history . . . make it difficult to speak other than of the faith (or faiths) of the *churches*' (italics original).[8]

He is correct to point out that 'since at least the sixteenth century, the churches of the West have had no single faith on any of these subjects [i.e. Baptism, Eucharist and Ministry].'[9]

As a consequence, Wright maintains, the most that a church can *fairly* be asked to do on reading *BEM* is to decide and declare whether the faith '*of its own tradition* in the Church through the ages' finds expression there. That is an acceptable alternative, but we may add that even if all the churches were able to answer *Wright's* question in the affirmative, that would not achieve much in terms of a *real* unity. It would be no more than a paper agreement and would yield only a paper church. But the question which *BEM* puts before the churches relates specifically to '*the faith*' of '*the Church*'.

What does this mean to those responsible for *BEM*? Wright declares that 'the question implies that behind the disagreements of the churches over the centuries there lurks a common faith on each of these thorny issues, which BEM claims to have unearthed and formulated.'[10]

While *BEM* is another example of ecumenical historiography and theology, Nissiotis regards it as expressing a *new* dimension in ecumenical thought and discussion. The preface to the report talks about 'a *kairos* of the ecumenical movement', i.e. something for which the time has come. He says that, because of a new factor and influence, 'separated church confessions, from the extreme Catholic side to the extreme Protestant one, can now together and in full agreement state items of faith on BEM which were not possible even a few years ago.'[11] What has brought about this change? Nissiotis writes:

> [It] is the new understanding of 'consensus' in a positive sense, i.e. confirming in common our basic elements of faith. We are being drawn into an act of '*consentire*', in the sense of being in a preliminary agreement by confessing in common the roots of our faith which are to be found in the Bible and the church life throughout the centuries. It is what in Greek one can characterize by the term '*koine synainesis*' which is a pleonasm (*koine* and *syn*) and which represents and undergirds the BEM text.[12]

Koine means 'common', and *syn* (or *sun*) means 'with' or 'together'. These terms attest to a 'common togetherness'. This is closely allied to, if not the same as, *sobornost*, the term which the Eastern Orthodox use for 'catholicity' or 'wholeness'. Applied to the church, it refers to a transcendent and indefinable

108

reality. Nissiotis, himself a person of Eastern Orthodox faith, declares that 'a great deal of the fuller ecumenical approach has been rightly attributed to the responsible and more active participation of Roman Catholic and Eastern Orthodox scholars in the actual drafting of the documents.'[13]

For the Ecumenical Movement to have become consciously conditioned by this ethos and approach means that a shift has occurred in its theological method. This change has involved a move away from the process of scientific examination and the inductive and deductive reasoning which go with it. Eastern Orthodoxy has complained long and loud about the prominence given to reasoning by Western theologians. Instead, it asserts the priority of the *apophatic* method, which means speaking of God and divine things by way of negation — that is, by saying what they are *not*. This method, it is claimed, is more suitable for speaking about divine *mysteries*. Now there is, of course, an apophatic element in God's self-revelation in Scripture — as, for example, in 'God is not man, that he should lie, or . . . repent' (Num. 23:19 RSV). However, this is accompanied in Scripture by an anthropomorphic element which paves the way for the reality of the incarnation. God's self-revelation is everywhere characterized by condescension to human beings — even to the use of human concepts and language forms. As His revelation is not contrary to reason, reasoning about it is not improper.

Given that the new-found *sense* of unity is of this kind, it is difficult, if not impossible, to subject it to biblical scrutiny and criticism. The indefinable becomes canonical. Nissiotis, therefore, claims that to approach statements like *BEM* in a proper manner requires '*a conversion of heart and mind* in order to confirm one's own confessional acts anew and *together with the other confessions within the one church* and biblical tradition' (italics mine).[14] The 'faith of the Church' is mainly the 'Church' as an object of faith — and the Church of the Ecumenical Movement at that.

What is the relationship between this 'faith' and *BEM*? Two different answers are given to this question within ecumenism, but a third element is already acting as a bridge between them. There are those who see *BEM* as a step towards agreement on one apostolic faith. Such stand broadly within the tradition derived from the Protestant Reformation. Others — and these are the Orthodox and the Catholics (both Roman Catholics and

Anglo-Catholics) — already see *BEM* as representing agreement in one apostolic faith. Lukas Vischer writes of this latter view:

> Everything the Church must confess and proclaim is already contained in them (i.e. in Baptism, Eucharist and Ministry) or at least indicated in them. In a certain sense, baptism, the Lord's Supper and the church structure willed by Christ are a summary of the Gospel . . . Agreement there, therefore, is already implicitly agreement in the understanding of the Gospel.[15]

After pointing out the gap between the two views outlined above, Vischer proceeds to construct a bridge over it. He states:

> The still-divided churches would be well advised, therefore, *to start living in accord with the agreement proposed by the Faith and Order Commission.* The more they let it guide their steps, the more they will discover that, basically, they are already one in the apostolic faith. The truth of the old maxim *lex orandi lex credendi* will be confirmed.[16]

This means that just as fellowship in ecumenism has generated the 'new' sense of oneness, so the practice of fellowship in accordance with *BEM* will make that oneness visible.

THE CONTENTS OF THE REPORT

BEM comprises numbered paragraphs in relation to each subject:

- Baptism (paras. 1-23).
- Eucharist (paras. 1-33).
- Ministry (paras. 1-55).

In these sections we find paragraphs of actual text *and* paragraphs of commentary. The former indicate 'the major areas of theological convergence' while the latter 'either indicate historical differences that have been overcome or identify disputed issues still in need of further research and reconciliation'.[17]

BEM, in our view, *countenances* sacramentalism and *accommodates* sacerdotalism. We have deliberately chosen the words which are in italics in the previous sentence. More should not be read into them than they actually say. At the same time we think that they *understate* the situation, but that will not be our main concern here. The criticism, as we originally expressed it above, is serious enough as it stands. With regard to baptism and the eucharist, the sign and the reality are so closely interrelated that grace can be found in the sign. With regard to ministry, the actions of a leader of a service are not utterly distinguished from those of a priest. Indeed, the term 'priest' is certainly not outlawed by this report. We shall now consider the report first of all in relation to *sacramentalism* and then in relation to *sacerdotalism*.

BEM AND SACRAMENTALISM

Under this heading we shall be examining what *BEM* says about baptism and the eucharist. We shall look at the subject of the eucharist first, because it is one to which we have already had to give some consideration (see chapter 2). It will give us the opportunity to link our comments here with our discussion of ARCIC 1 in that chapter.

Dr Roger Beckwith regards the Lima report on the eucharist as 'a very confused and confusing text'.[18] He explains this partly by referring to its historical background and development. He writes:

> Like the Lima statement on Baptism, it was originally brought together by the extraordinary method of collecting anything that the four World Conferences on Faith and Order and the first four General Assemblies of the World Council of Churches had said which related to the subject and trying to arrange these scattered utterances in some sort of order. This was done at Louvain in 1971.[19]

A particular (and serious) source of confusion is bound up with the idea of anamnesis. Beckwith points out that Lima assumes what ARCIC I declares, namely, that 'Christ's body and blood are present at holy communion not just in the reception of the sacrament, but from the consecration of the elements onwards'.[20] This is all of a piece with Orthodox theology, as the *Anglican-Orthodox dialogue: the Moscow Agreed Statement* makes clear.[21] In addition, Beckwith states that, according to *BEM*, the eucharist refers to 'Christ himself with all that he has accomplished for us and for all creation (in his incarnation, servanthood, ministry, teaching, suffering, sacrifice, resurrection, ascension and sending of the Spirit).'[22] Beckwith adds, 'The New Testament emphasis that the sacramental commemoration

111

"proclaims Christ's *death*" (1 Corinthians 11:26) is here quite lost to view.'[23]

This is not trifling detail. It points to a particular 'world view' of the sacraments. Gerald Bray writes: 'The most fundamental controversy surrounding the sacraments is that of the *res significata* [i.e. the thing signified].'[24]

What do the sacraments signify or point to? Bray lists three answers which are given to this question, namely, the incarnation (Catholic view), the atonement (Orthodox/Protestant view) and the kingdom (the view of many New Testament scholars). After acknowledging that these views cannot be rigidly compartmentalized, he goes on to say: 'What matters . . . is the emphasis, since this will determine the understanding which will be attached to the sacraments.'[25]

The emphasis of *BEM* is patently not on the atonement. The excerpt already quoted makes it clear that the death of Christ is but one item among others to which the eucharist relates. This, however, is not the limit to which this shift goes. It is taken beyond other 'moments' in the Christ-event. We read: 'The eucharist embraces all aspects of life. It is a representative act of thanksgiving and offering on behalf of the whole world'.[26]

Again, *BEM* declares:

> [The Eucharist] is the great thanksgiving to the Father for everything accomplished in creation, redemption and sanctification, for everything accomplished by God now in the Church and in the world in spite of the sins of human beings, for everything that God will accomplish in bringing the Kingdom to fulfilment.[27]

This is akin to the Orthodox view, which sees the whole of life as sacramental. In this sacramental theology the atoning death of Christ is no longer given pride of place. Bray is absolutely correct when he says:

> Remove the atonement from the centre of discussion and a consensus is possible *on a different basis*. Sacramental fellowship can then be renewed without resolving the theological problems which caused the split in the first place.
>
> This practice, which is described in ecumenical dialogue as 'an escape from past controversies by transposing the discussion to a different level' is ingenious but evasive. It does not solve problems of theological principle but merely relativizes them so that sacramental practice need not be affected. Sooner or later, however, an agreement at this superficial level is bound to fail.[28]

The section of *BEM* entitled 'The Meaning of the Eucharist' examines the subject under five subheadings. These are:

- 'The Eucharist as Thanksgiving to the Father'
- 'The Eucharist as Anamnesis or Memorial of Christ'
- 'The Eucharist as Invocation of the Spirit'
- 'The Eucharist as Communion of the Faithful'
- 'The Eucharist as Meal of the Kingdom'

From the point of view of sacramentalism, it is the second and third elements which really matter. We shall proceed to examine them under the headings of 'Anamnesis' and 'Epiclesis'.

Dr Wright asserts that Lima 'tends to overstate the role of the Eucharist within the whole economy of the Christian faith. It could be accused of para-eucharisticism.' He adds that 'most sections couple some biblically-based material with a tendency to exaggerate the importance of the sacrament'.[29] To claim that it is 'the central act of the Church's worship' begs the question of the nature and place of a sacrament in the life of the church. But such imprecision is the kind of soil in which sacramentalism is not only found but where it can also flourish.

Anamnesis

We shall not examine this subject in detail here since we have already given some consideration to it in chapter 2 (see pp. 74-8). We must, however, note that, like ARCIC I, *BEM* sees the idea of 'memorial' as providing a 'breakthrough in the problems of eucharistic theology'. The Lima report repeatedly translates anamnesis as 'memorial' rather than 'remembrance'. It defines it as follows: 'The biblical idea of memorial as applied to the eucharist refers to this present efficacy of God's work [i.e. in the incarnate, crucified and risen Christ] when it is celebrated by God's people in a liturgy.'[30]

Dr Wright correctly sees the result of such a construction as being 'more our reminding God than our remembering, more the making present of the past than the remembrance or commemoration of it and hence the actualisation of the sacrifice of the cross in the sacrament itself.'[31]

Beckwith detects what lies behind this incorrect understanding of anamnesis and is responsible for it. It is, he says, 'speculation about the relationship between Christianity and the mystery religions by Dom Odo Cassel, popularized in the English-speaking world by Dom Gregory Dix (in his *Shape of the Liturgy*) and by other liturgiologists and theologians'.[32] His verdict is that 'this pagan Greek notion has, quite incongruously, been read into the Jewish passover'.[33]

All that has been said in chapter 2 in opposition to this view of anamnesis is relevant here. Such a view lacks Old Testament and New Testament *exegetical* support. It diverts attention from Christ's finished work on the cross to something which a priest does on an altar or a table (and which the church is therefore able to do), namely, offer Christ. The 'commentary paragraph' in this section on anamnesis seeks to commend the Roman Catholic error of 'propitiatory sacrifice' on this basis of reminding God of Christ's work on the cross. It is, therefore, inimical to the gospel. We must note here that *BEM* places this idea of the real presence and offering to God firmly in the centre of ecumenical eucharistic theology. This indicates the triumph of the Catholic view (i.e. Roman, Orthodox and Anglo-Catholic) over the Protestant. Such thinking points unmistakably in a sacramentalist direction in spite of the acknowledgement of differences as to how to understand and express this mystery.[34]

Epiclesis

The mention of epiclesis in *BEM* reinforces our argument about its sacramental tendency. The report declares that 'the whole action of the eucharist has an "epikletic" character because it depends upon the work of the Holy Spirit.'[35]

Epiclesis is a Greek term which means 'calling on'. The Person who is called on, or invoked, is the Holy Spirit. In the liturgy of the Eastern Orthodox churches, the Spirit is believed to descend on the bread and wine at the eucharist in response to this invocation. Epiclesis is regarded by the Orthodox as absolutely crucial for the validity of their sacrament.

It is true, of course, that the Spirit's ministry is vital, if any benefit is to be gained not only from the eucharist, but also from baptism or any other element in public worship. However, the work of the Holy Spirit in connection with the eucharist could be described without any mention of epiclesis. The inclusion of the term in *BEM*, therefore, is an indication of the powerful influence of Eastern Orthodox theology and of the highly sacramental character of the ecumenical eucharist.

Both the Roman Catholic Church and the Eastern Orthodox churches believe the sacraments *contain* grace. Yet, as far as the eucharist is concerned, the Holy Spirit's ministry does *not* consist of effecting a change of any kind in the elements of bread and wine. What He does is to affect the believer, the one who is the recipient of the bread and wine. *BEM* declares quite correctly: 'The Spirit makes the crucified and risen Christ really present to us in the eucharistic meal . . . [He is] the One who makes the historical words of Jesus present and alive . . . [He makes] the eucharistic event . . . a reality.'[36]

Sacraments without the Holy Spirit can never, ever become means of grace. But is this what *BEM* means by the 'epikletic character' of the eucharist? The answer which *BEM* gives to such a question is that it is through epiclesis that the bread and wine *become* the body and blood of Christ. The statement declares: 'It is in virtue of the living word of Christ and by the power of the Holy Spirit that the bread and wine become the sacramental signs of Christ's body and blood.'[37]

The Spirit, therefore, is responsible for this 'becoming'. It will be noted that the above extract does not say 'become *to us*', but 'become'. The recipient is not in view at all. The elements have become something in themselves quite apart from the communicant or the communing. The above quotation continues: 'They remain so [i.e. as the body and blood] for the purpose of communion.'[38] There will doubtless be a disclaimer that this 'becoming' means a material change, but this is not the charge which we are making. Our charge is levelled rather against the view that the bread and wine *become anything* other than bread and wine.

BEM places great emphasis on this invocation of the Spirit. Commentary paragraph 14 refers to traditions which relate this to 'a special moment of consecration'.[39] This is of course a reference to Eastern Orthodoxy and (by implication) to Roman Catholicism as well. *BEM* does not enlarge on this. Since the liturgy of the Orthodox is not widely known in the West and its significance therefore not appreciated, we shall here include a lengthy quotation from an Orthodox writer on the subject.

Timothy Ware (also known as Father Kallistos) is an Orthodox priest and monk. In a book about his Church, he describes the Orthodox eucharist. He defines anamnesis as 'the act of "calling to mind" and "offering".' He goes on to say what takes place after anamnesis:

Then comes the Epiclesis, as a rule read secretly, but sometimes in full hearing of the congregation. 'Send down Thy Holy Spirit upon us and upon these gifts here set forth:

And make this bread the Precious Body of Thy Christ,
And that which is in this cup, the Precious Blood of Thy Christ,
Changing them by Thy Holy Spirit. Amen. Amen. Amen.'

Priest and deacon immediately prostrate themselves before the Holy Gifts, which have now been consecrated.

It will be evident that the 'moment of consecration' is understood somewhat differently by the Orthodox and the Roman Catholic Churches. According to Latin theology, the consecration is effected by the Words of Institution: 'This is my Body . . .' 'This is my Blood . . .' According to Orthodox theology, the act of consecration is not complete until the end of the Epiklesis, and worship of the Holy Gifts before this point is condemned by the Orthodox Church as 'aritolatry' (bread worship). Orthodox, however, do not teach that consecration is effected *solely* by the *Epiklesis*, nor do they regard the Words of Institution as incidental and unimportant. On the contrary, they look upon the entire Eucharistic Prayer as forming a single and individual whole, so that the true main sections of the prayer — Thanksgiving, Anamnesis, Epiklesis — all form an integral part of the one act of consecration. But this, of course, means that if we are to single out 'a moment of consecration', such a moment cannot come until the *Amen* of the *Epiklesis*.[40]

These words point to and express a change in the elements which is no less real than their visible appearance and tangibility. That the scholastic theory of transubstantiation is rejected is immaterial. The bread and wine become in themselves the body and blood of Christ. This is what *BEM* is teaching, and Wright is generous to see what it says on this point as 'a half unsuccessful attempt to break out of the confines of Catholic and Orthodox tradition'.[41]

Faith

There is no doubt that *BEM* insists on the doctrine of the Real Presence, which means that when the bread and wine somehow become Christ's body and blood, grace is contained in the sacrament. In view of this insistence, only one thing can save *BEM* from having to succumb to the charge of sacramentalism. It is that the document contains a strong emphasis on the nature and necessity of *faith*. It stresses that faith must be present if grace is

116

to be received. We shall therefore seek to discover what *BEM* says on this matter of faith.

Those who partake of the eucharist are variously described in *BEM*. From the standpoint of what the document says about faith, the two expressions which are most directly relevant are 'the faithful' and the 'believer[s]'. As these terms are traditional expressions of Catholicism and Protestantism respectively, they are not precise enough to settle what *BEM* teaches about faith. The report's statement that the elements are to be offered to the Father 'in faith' does not help us very much. What is this 'faith'?

Two other expressions should be noted. They are 'justified sinners' and 'baptized members of the body of Christ'. With regard to the first of these, the report uses this expression only once,[42] does not distinguish it from sanctification and does not connect it with faith (see chapter 3). The expression 'baptized members' is much more important for our inquiry, because it links baptism with the eucharist. Our inquiry about faith in relation to the eucharist must therefore include what is said about it in relation to baptism, particularly as baptism usually precedes the eucharist.

Baptism and faith

Before pursuing our task, we will examine *BEM* to see whether its treatment of baptism is open to the same charge of sacramentalism as its treatment of the eucharist. We are in no doubt that it is and that ecumenists make much of what they term 'one common baptism'.

Given the presence of Baptists in the WCC, it is inevitable that their beliefs and practice should be taken into account in this document. (We must not, however, overlook the fact that immersion is the practice of Orthodox churches, even for infants.) In our view, the disagreement between paedobaptist and non-paedobaptist churches does not of necessity touch on the content of the gospel, and so we shall not here enter into a discussion of what *BEM* has to say on that dispute. It is, however, worth noting that the report warns very mildly against the practice of indiscriminate infant baptism and favours believers' baptism as that which is plainly found in the New Testament. *BEM* declares: 'While the possibility that infant baptism was also practised in the apostolic age cannot be excluded, baptism upon personal profession of faith is the most clearly attested pattern in the New Testament documents.'[43] This evidence, however, does not settle the matter because of the influence of Tradition in paedobaptist ecumenical churches.

Since our first task is to see whether *BEM*'s statements about baptism give substance to the charge of sacramentalism, we shall need to consider the following quotations:

> [Christian baptism] is incorporation into Christ, who is the crucified and risen Lord; it is entry into the New Covenant between God and God's people. (para. 1)

> Baptism initiates the reality of the new life given in the midst of the present world. (para. 7)

> God bestows upon all baptized persons the anointing and promise of the Holy Spirit, marks them with a seal and implants in their hearts the first instalment of their inheritance as sons and daughters of God. (para. 5)[44]

The emphasis in these statements is plainly on the efficacy of baptism. The mood and tense of the verbs in the above excerpts are important. Something is achieved by means of baptism.

The last quotation links the Holy Spirit with baptism in much the same way as epiclesis connects the activity of the Spirit with the eucharist. Though the influence of the 'Catholic' strain is again quite noticeable at this point, there is no unanimity as to what supplies the sign of the gift of the Spirit in baptism. For some, it is the water. For others, it is the anointing with oil (charismation) or the laying on of hands. This variety is analogous to the differing explanations of how the Real Presence is effected in the eucharist. Yet the differences are no longer regarded by ecumenists as vital. This is because the facts of Christ's presence in the eucharist and the Spirit's agency in baptism are matters of common belief and are asserted with equal vigour with regard to both sacraments. They are also interconnected. *BEM* declares:

> In God's work of salvation, the paschal mystery of Christ's death and resurrection is inseparably linked with the pentecostal gift of the Holy Spirit. Similarly, participation in Christ's death and resurrection is inseparably linked with the receiving of the Spirit. Baptism in its full meaning signifies and *effects* both [italics mine].[45]

From all this (namely, paragraphs 2-7 of the section on baptism) we believe it is fair to conclude that *BEM* countenances baptismal regeneration. The teaching is highly realistic and consonant with the *ex opere operato* dogma of the Council of Trent. Dr David Wright comments: 'Acute questions have been raised about their affirmations, which appear to speak both of meaning and efficacy, as though every baptism invariably conferred the benefits spelt out here.'[46] He refers to a paper by Colin Buchanan who has declared: 'There has to be a *credibility* to our statements on baptism and the high-sounding and marvellous claims of [this section] can only be sustained by hedging their unqualified appearance with some qualifications about the conditions under which baptism is truly efficacious.'[47] Buchanan believes that paragraphs 8-10 of *BEM* (entitled 'Baptism and Faith') provide these qualifications. Wright agrees with him and says: 'When the statements on "The Meaning of Baptism" are taken within the context of the Baptism section as a whole, they cannot be read as favouring any notion of the automatic conferral of new life whether of infants or believers.'[48]

We do not share this certainty at all because of the way in which this document speaks about faith. We shall therefore consider paragraphs 8-10 which bear the title 'Baptism and Faith'. What is obvious from a cursory reading of these three paragraphs is that two of them (paras. 9-10) refer to the life and growth of faith *subsequent* to baptism. It is in this setting that the expression 'baptised believers' is found. These paragraphs are therefore not strictly relevant to the nature of faith and to its necessity for the purpose of baptism. It is paragraph 8 alone which is relevant, and we shall here quote it in full:

> Baptism is both God's gift and our human response to that gift. It looks towards a growth into the measure of the stature of the fullness of Christ (Eph. 4:13). The necessity of faith for the reception of the salvation embodied and set forth in baptism is acknowledged by all churches. Personal commitment is necessary for responsible membership in the body of Christ.[49]

Clearly, the third sentence in this paragraph is the crucial one. It seems to say all that needs to be said about the necessity of faith for baptism to be efficacious under the good hand of God. We must, however, make two observations about this. First of all, *the nature of faith is not defined* and secondly, *the reference to all the churches makes that omission significant.*

119

To mention faith without defining it is to use a word without agreeing about its meaning. What is more, all the churches do *not* agree about the nature of faith. The Reformation debate about faith being assent or trust (persuasion) is not referred to, let alone resolved. This is vital to the doctrine of the sacraments, because the Roman Catholic Church teaches that faith means not putting an obstacle in the way of the efficacy of the sacraments. This sentence about the necessity of faith neither asserts what is necessary nor denies what is erroneous.

One paragraph, which does not belong to this section on baptism and faith, is also relevant here. It is paragraph 4. It begins as follows:

> The baptism which makes Christians partakers of the mystery of Christ's death and resurrection implies confession of sin and conversion of heart. The baptism administered by John was itself a baptism of repentance for the forgiveness of sins (Mark 1:4).[50]

Does this statement not serve the purpose? It is certainly a clearer statement about the nature of faith and repentance from sin. Again, however, we must bear in mind the composition of ecumenism. Confession of sin is mentioned, but to whom is it to be made? To God or to a priest? And what is repentance? Does it mean the same to a Roman Catholic as it does to a person of baptist persuasion?

In addition, the word 'implies' in the quotation is rather weak. 'Requires' would be better in order to place emphasis on 'confession of sin and conversion of heart'. But the emphasis in paragraph 4 is on baptism and not on faith or conversion, as the concluding sentence of this paragraph makes clear:

> Those baptized are pardoned, cleansed and sanctified by Christ, and are given as part of their baptismal experience a new ethical orientation under the guidance of the Holy Spirit.[51]

Evangelicals would substitute 'believing' for 'baptized' and its cognate term in this statement. Baptism is certainly vital for salvation in ecumenical theology. While *BEM* refers to baptism as a sign, it is never *merely* a sign. It is so related to the reality that the possibility of sign without the reality (baptism without faith) is never considered, nor is the reverse (being saved without being baptized).

Eucharist and faith

Much the same can be said about eucharist and faith. The important statement here is: 'While Christ's real presence in the eucharist does not depend on the faith of the individual, all agree that to discern the body and blood of Christ, faith is required.'[52]

This means that Christ is present in the bread and wine whether the communicant has faith or not. Furthermore, faith is necessary only to discern or perceive. It is not essential in order to partake and thus obtain benefit. Faith is again demoted and the sacrament elevated. On the matter of the eucharist, Wright is correct, if rather mild, when he says: 'Whereas this report, with its anamnesis and epiklesis and its long list of standard elements for the observance of the eucharist, seems to be moving towards a more complex tradition-laden ecclesiasticization of the sacraments, evangelical churchmen will aspire after a greater biblical simplicity.'[53] That biblical simplicity means denying that the elements become in themselves anything other than bread and wine, that Christ's body is anywhere other than in heaven, and that anything is offered to the Father but thanks. The gratitude that we express is for what Christ did on the cross to purchase our salvation, what He offers to us as believers by His Spirit by means of the reminders of bread and wine, and what He will bring and do when He comes again.

Baptism: New Testament evidence and its interpretation

One other aspect of this matter must be dealt with before we come to what *BEM* has to say about ministry. It relates to the kind of language used in the New Testament with regard to baptism. Wright says:

> Modern evangelical theology has often spoken of baptism (and also communion) as *symbolizing* new life in Christ. It has preferred to speak in terms of signification or even representation rather than of baptism actually effecting what it signifies. Although the Lima document refers to baptism several times as a sign . . . it commonly uses realist language as though baptism confers what it signifies. Such a way of speaking about the Christian sacraments is more in line with the usage of the New Testament.[54]

Before we look at the New Testament language, we ought to state that the question of its interpretation is not the major dispute evangelicals ought to have with *BEM*, and much less ought such language to forge a link between ecumenical sacramental theology and evangelical teaching. We must not forget that in *BEM*, grace is located in the sacraments. Faith is relegated and its nature left unclear. While it is possible to live with the teaching that the sacraments effect what they signify when they are properly administered and when the way of salvation remains intact, this is not possible in an ecumenical setting.

But what of this New Testament language and its interpretation? Herman Ridderbos discusses this in his work entitled *Paul: an Outline of his Theology*. The relevant section is called 'Baptism as Means of Salvation'. He sums up the New Testament evidence as follows:

> Baptism is . . . the means by which communion with the death and burial of Christ comes into being (Rom. 6:4), the place where this union is effected (. . . Col. 2:12), the means by which Christ cleanses his church (. . . Eph. 5:26), and God has saved it (. . . Tit. 3:5) so that baptism itself can be called the washing of regeneration and of the renewing by the Holy Spirit (Tit. 3:5). All these formulations speak clearly of the significance of baptism in mediating redemption.[55]

He continues in a very assertive and explicit manner:

> [These formulations] speak of what happens in and by baptism and not merely of what happened before baptism and of which baptism would only be the confirmation.[56]

Having said this, Ridderbos goes on to emphasize faith and its priority. He declares:

> On the other hand, it is plain from all his preaching that baptism, as means of salvation, does not have an exclusive significance. Thus what is here attributed to baptism can elsewhere be ascribed to faith . . . And thus what is here represented as appropriated to [by?] believers by baptism can elsewhere be ascribed to them already in Christ's death as the proof of God's love and as the reconciliation with God accomplished in him (Rom. 5:8, 10).[57]

(This must mean that a person can be in Christ and therefore saved without being baptized, but Ridderbos does not say this in as many words in this section.)

What is to be deduced from this presentation of two foci — namely, faith and baptism — instead of one, Ridderbos sums up as follows:

> We can draw no other conclusion than that baptism accomplishes in its own way what already obtained in another way, and thus occupies its own place in the whole of the divine communication of redemption.[58]

Clearly, something is regarded as being accomplished or appropriated in baptism. It is not something *connected* with salvation, but rather *identical* to it — that is, the thing itself. This is not easy to understand. To say the least, it is potentially dangerous, because it not only leads to the possibility of salvation being received at two different points, but it also results in two ways of salvation. That would be disastrous for the gospel.

We must, however, note the expression 'in its own way . . . and . . . place' and study what Ridderbos conceives this to be. In his view, this does not mean that baptism unites to the church whereas faith does not, much less that baptism makes actual what is possible in Christ's death. For Ridderbos, Christ did something on the cross and this is received by faith, but baptism also does something in its own right. What is this? Ridderbos takes the view that the theological setting for baptism is the application of redemption. He says: 'It is in the framework of this individualizing application of what once happened in Christ that baptism has a place as the divine promise and appropriation of salvation, and as the believer allowing himself to be invested with it.'[59]

Two comments are in order here. The first is that in this statement there is a shift away from considering the 'moments' of faith and of baptism and their inter-relationship. The subject has now become *being in Christ and faith/baptism*. There is a lack of integration here. Secondly, we must ask whether faith without baptism is a valid way of receiving salvation, even if it is granted that all believers should be baptized. Or is faith plus baptism necessary? In response, we would make the following points:

1. Faith alone is more than enough to receive the whole of salvation. Failure to assert this unequivocally means that too much is being given to baptism in the scheme of salvation.

2. Once people make such a claim for faith apart from baptism as the means of receiving the salvation which is in Christ, it becomes vital to examine the question of the New Testament's language on the subject. We propose the following way of inter-

preting those statements — a way which, we venture to believe, does justice to this teaching. We shall point to the fact that the New Testament speaks of baptism without referring to water at all (Rom. 6:3,4) and speaks of water or washing in connection with the *word* rather than baptism (Eph. 5:26). The underlying truth in these passages is the 'baptism' of the Spirit (1 Cor. 12:13) who uses the word to regenerate, to cleanse from the past and to create the soul anew (Ezek. 36:25; John 3:5 and Titus 3:5). In this light, one can speak as unreservedly about the efficacy of baptism as one can about the necessity of faith. Indeed, the former produces the latter. Regeneration joins the soul to Christ *unconsciously*. Faith unites the soul to Him *consciously*. Baptism in water is the declaration of this in a public way. In our view, it is not only with regard to the eucharist that *BEM* speaks too highly, but also with regard to baptism. The Reformed constituency would do well to remember the following statement by William Cunningham:

> We have no doubt that the general tendency among Protestant divines, both at the period of the Reformation and in the seventeenth century, was to lean to the side of magnifying the value and efficacy of the sacraments, and that some of the statements even in the symbolical books of some churches, are not altogether free from indications of this kind.[60]

BEM AND SACERDOTALISM

We turn finally — and much more briefly — to what the Lima report has to say on the subject of the ministry. In doing so, our aim will be to see whether or not it excludes sacerdotalism (a word which derives from the Latin *sacerdos* meaning 'priest'). We shall, therefore, be concentrating on what is said about the priesthood in this document. Though the report begins with the subject 'The Calling of the Whole People of God', it looks at it in very general terms and devotes only six paragraphs to the matter. The remaining forty-eight paragraphs concentrate on 'The Church and the Ordained Ministry'. This imbalance lends weight to Wright's declaration that 'it is precisely this virtual identification between Ministry and ordained personnel that has to be exposed and overthrown.'[61] However, given the composition of the WCC, this preoccupation with the ordained ministry is inevitable, especially as there are deep disagreements over the forms it takes. Since the priesthood is bound up with ordination, we must include episcopacy in our study of what the report says about the ministry.

The term 'priest' occurs in this document before the term 'bishop'. There may be no great significance in that. It is, however, an indication of how vital it is in ecumenical circles to find some way of retaining the term and to justify a form of a ministry to which the term may be applied. There is no possibility of the Ecumenical Movement restricting the use of the word 'priest' to references to Christ and His people. We therefore find that this word is introduced and sanctioned at an early stage in *BEM*. Its retention is argued for on the basis that when it is used of the ordained ministry the terminology 'differs in appropriate ways from the sacrificial priesthood of the Old Testament, from the unique redemptive priesthood of Christ and from the corporate priesthood of the people of God'.[62]

The document then seeks to support this view by a reference to Romans 15:16. There Paul describes his ministry as a 'priestly service' (RSV). But even this argument from the New Testament fails, because Paul calls the Christians at Philippi to engage in a similar kind of service in offering themselves to God (Phil. 2:17 — the Greek term is *leitourgia*). There is therefore no avoiding the stubborn fact that the New Testament provides no help to those who want to use 'priestly' terms to describe the activities of the ordained ministry in any exclusive sense.

The other justification offered by *BEM* for using such language of the ordained is grounded on the work they do. This is discussed as follows:

> They may appropriately be called priests because they fulfil a particular priestly service by strengthening and building up the royal and prophetic priesthood of the faithful through word and sacraments, through their prayers of intercession, and through their pastoral guidance of the community.[63]

All these expressions could describe the work of a pastor/teacher in a non-episcopal church. There is therefore not only no *New Testament* justification for speaking of priesthood in relation to ministry, but also no need to do so in order to describe what is involved in such ministry. The need derives only from the desire to include Roman Catholic and Orthodox teaching on the matter. It is sacramentalism which creates the need for sacerdotal language.

Episcopacy

As the existence of bishops is necessary for the ordination of priests/presbyters, the report is emphatic about the need for them in the Church. Paragraph 23 declares:

> A ministry of *episkopé* is necessary to express and safeguard the unity of the body. Every church needs this ministry of unity **in some form** in order to be the Church of God, the one body of Christ, a sign of the unity of all in the Kingdom.[64]

The words in bold type (the emphasis is mine) leave room for the fact that non-episcopalian churches may have a 'ministry of *episcopé*' (pastoral oversight) but in a different form. This is explicitly acknowledged later in the report (para. 53b). However, the threefold ministry of bishops, priests and deacons is still urged upon such churches. Indeed, the report does this in spite of the fact that the New Testament does not mention it (acknowledged in paras. 19-25) and actually contradicts it by identifying the word 'bishop' with 'elder' (a term to which the report makes no reference at all). *BEM* recognizes that the threefold ministry is in need of some reform in order to accommodate the principle of collegiality and to emphasize the importance of diaconal ministry. Nevertheless, the report sees no way in which this threefold ministry can be jettisoned. It is rather the case that its potential 'for the most effective witness of the Church in this world' has not been realized.[65]

The reason why the threefold ministry is defended so vigorously is because of the status and role of the bishops in the life of the church.

> [Bishops are] representative pastoral ministers of oversight, continuity and unity in the Church . . . They serve the apostolicity and unity of the Church's teaching, worship and sacramental life. They have responsibility for leadership in the Church's mission. They relate the Christian community in their area to the wider Church, and the universal Church to their community. They, in communion with the presbyters and deacons and the whole community, are responsible for the orderly transfer of ministerial authority in the Church.[66]

The theology of apostolic succession lies behind this statement and a section of *BEM* is given over to it (paras. 34-38). It is entitled 'Succession in the Apostolic Tradition'. While this tradi-

126

tion includes 'the Gospel and the life of the community'[67], the bishops have a crucial role in its transmission through 'apostolic succession'. The report declares: 'This succession was understood as serving, symbolizing and guarding the continuity of the apostolic faith and communion.'[68] *BEM* is altogether too sanguine in its view of bishops and their role. While acknowledging that the succession is not 'a guarantee' of the continuity of the apostolic tradition, it genuinely seems to believe that 'churches which have not retained the episcopate' but have their own ministry of oversight do 'appreciate the episcopal succession as a sign . . . of the continuity and unity of the Church.'[69] While many involved in ecumenical negotiations may look upon episcopal succession in this way, should evangelicals so regard it when departure from apostolic teaching recorded in the Scriptures has been authorized by bishops themselves? As Wright declares: 'Episcopacy does not have a very impressive track record as an agent of the historical continuity of the apostolic tradition, nor in the present day has its performance in safeguarding the apostolic faith been at all noteworthy.'[70]

Given what lies behind this deliberately understated objection, evangelical churches will find great difficulty with the following request which *BEM* makes of them:

> [They] are asked to realize that the continuity with the Church of the apostles finds profound expression in the successive laying on of hands by bishops and that, though they may not lack the continuity of the apostolic tradition, this sign will strengthen and deepen that continuity. They may need to recover the sign of the episcopal succession.[71]

Various kinds of responses to this statement come to mind. We will restrict ourselves to one. Given that evangelicals have the tradition (that is to say, the apostolic deposit, teaching and gospel), why should they submit to a sign from those who lack that reality?

Priesthood

Our main concern in examining what is said about ministry in *BEM* is to note what it says about the priesthood. We have already observed that it argues strongly for the retention and use of the term to describe the ministry of those who are neither bishops nor deacons. The terms 'minister', 'presbyter' or 'priest' are therefore interchangeable and this needs to be borne in mind whenever we read about ministers or presbyters. Old priests are new presbyters writ large. We have also noted that bishops are vital to the ordination process, that is, the making of priests/presbyters.

Ordination is the conferring of that gift of the Holy Spirit, which is suited to the kind of ministry to which a person is being appointed — whether it be as a bishop, priest or deacon. An appropriate authority is also conveyed. While this authority is defined functionally, as in the case of Scripture, and its use modelled after the example of Christ, it is not dependent on or conditioned by the opinions of the community.

With regard to the priesthood (we will now keep to this term), men are set apart to be 'pastoral ministers of Word and sacraments in a local eucharistic community.'[72] This statement links the priest with the eucharist quite explicity, and we must inquire into anything that is said about this role in that connection. Paragraph 14 is the relevant statement on this subject. It reads:

> It is especially in the eucharistic celebration that the ordained ministry is the visible focus of the deep and all-embracing communion between Christ and the members of his body. In the celebration of the eucharist, Christ gathers, teaches, and nourishes the Church. It is Christ who invites to this meal and who presides at it. In most churches this presidency is signified and represented by an ordained minister.[73]

In considering this statement, it is vital to do two things. The first is to substitute the word 'priest' for 'ordained minister'. It is perfectly legitimate to do this and, indeed, most necessary given the composition of the group which drew up and subscribed this document. It would be a great mistake for a Baptist to read this statement and think only of his denomination. Secondly, we must call to mind what has already been written on the subject of the eucharist both in the second chapter of this volume as well as in the present chapter.

It will be remembered that an offering of Christ is made to God in the eucharist, as it is understood in ecumenical circles. By means of this offering, the sacrifice of Christ is re-presented (made present all over again) together with its benefits in the context of the church. The above declaration from paragraph 14 of *BEM* makes it clear that this is done through an ordained minister. This is a doctrine of the priesthood described under the term 'minister'.

The pastor/teacher does not symbolize or represent Christ (i.e. make Him present). He is not 'the visible focus' of communion between Christ and the church, let alone 'especially' so. It is the priest who is an *alter Christus* — another Christ, or, Christ in another form. To speak of the minister in this way is almost to speak of another mediator, only this time between Christ and the church. It does not exclude sacerdotalism.

Baptism, Eucharist and Ministry definitely countenances sacramentalism and, in an equally definite manner, does not exclude sacerdotalism. The two form a potent mixture which can only corrupt the gospel. Sacramentalism and sacerdotalism do not produce true spirituality. Their offspring has been Protestant sentimentality and Catholic superstition.

5
Mission and Evangelism

In this chapter we shall continue our study of ecumenical ecclesiology by giving particular attention to the church's task in the world. As the World Council of Churches sees it, a close link exists between the nature of the church and what it regards as her task:

> As the churches grow into unity, they are asking how their understandings, and practices of baptism, eucharist and ministry relate to their mission in and for the renewal of the human community as they seek to promote justice, peace and reconciliation. Therefore our understanding of these cannot be divorced from the redemptive and liberating mission of Christ through the churches in the modern world.[1]

The WCC's view of the role the church in the world will help us to understand the direction in which the Council appears to be going.

In a very real sense the WCC owes its origin to the missionary movement of the nineteenth century. That movement was responsible for the calling of the International Missionary Conference held in Edinburgh in 1910. In its turn, the conference brought about the emergence of the Faith and Order Movement, which was constituted in 1920, and the Life and Work Movement ten years after that. H.P. Van Dusen has written: 'At virtually every point, the conviction and impulses of Christian unity originated within the enterprise of Christian mission'.[2]

The Edinburgh conference was directly responsible for bringing into being the International Missionary Council (IMC for short). The latter continued as a distinct organization after 1948, when the WCC was formally constituted at Amsterdam and both the Faith and Order and the Life and Work Movements became departments within the WCC. At the 1958 IMC conference in Ghana, it was proposed that the IMC should also become a department of the WCC. This took place at the 1961 assembly of the WCC in New Delhi. The IMC then became the CWME (Commission on World Mission and Evangelism). This story and its sequel is important as part of the development of the WCC's theology of mission. It is told with astounding frankness and detail by Harvey Hoekstra in his book *Evangelism in Eclipse: World Mission and the World Council of Churches.*[3] We shall be quoting from this work in the course of this chapter.

Evangelism is, of course, at the heart of evangelicalism, as the term indicates. It also lies at the heart of ecumenism. Because this is so, and because the churches of the Third World are active in the WCC , evangelism cannot provide a clear line of demarcation between the WCC on the one hand, and the Lausanne Congress on World Evangelisation (LCWE) together with the World Evangelical Fellowship (WEF) on the other. The challenge that the contemporary world presents to mission has therefore been considered by evangelicals too. While we shall concentrate on ecumenical documents, we shall also have occasion to allude to evangelical ones.

We take as our starting point the WCC statement entitled *Mission and Evangelism: an Ecumenical Affirmation.*[4] From now on we shall refer to this publication as *M & E*. This document was the result of a request which was made after the 1975 WCC assembly in Nairobi. The request was that the CWME should 'prepare a document setting forth the basic convictions of the ecumenical movement on the topic of mission and evangelism'. This was discussed before, during and after the Melbourne Conference of 1980. The result was that *M & E* was submitted to the Central Committee of the WCC in 1982. It was approved and remitted to the churches.

Like the Faith and Order Commission, the CWME is made up of representatives of the various church traditions found within the WCC, including representatives from the Roman Catholic Church. This document should therefore be studied against that varied background. Dr Emilio Castro, the director of CWME, writes in its foreword:

> We hope this document makes explicit the underlying convictions of the World Council of Churches and is helpful to member churches as an outline of our common understandings in the vital area of mission and evangelism.[5]

We will assume that, as all member churches were consulted before the document was approved and had their comments taken into consideration, *M & E* may be regarded as an officially agreed statement.

'MISSION' AND 'MISSIONS'

M & E is not a lengthy document. It is made up of a preface, 47 paragraphs of main text, correlated with 11 paragraphs of explanatory appendices. The main section is subdivided under the following heads:

- The call to mission (paras. 1-5)
- The call to proclamation and witness (6-8)
- Ecumenical convictions (9)
- Conversion (10-13)
- The gospel's application to all realms of life (14-19)
- The church and its unity in God's mission (20-27)
- Mission in Christ's way (28-30)
- Good News to the poor (31-36)
- Mission in and to six continents (37-40)
- Witness among people of living faiths (41-45)
- Looking towards the future (46-47)

Before selecting some of these subjects for individual consideration we must look at the statement generally and seek to set it in its historical and theological context. To do this, we shall focus on the term 'mission', which appears in the title of the document. What is *mission* in ecumenical parlance?

The term dates back to the 1960s. Hoekstra writes about this period as follows: 'The winds of change were blowing. So strong were they that the "s" was blown right off the word "missions". The term *missions* became *mission*. Only later would many realize that much more than a change in spelling was involved'.[6]

Bishop Lesslie Newbigin referred to this change at the time, and entered a plea for the retention of the older term along with the newer one. He wrote:

> When we speak of 'the mission of the church' we mean everything that the church is sent into the world to do . . . But within this totality there is a narrower concern which we usually speak of as 'missions'. Let us, without being too refined, define the narrower concern by saying: it is the concern that in the places where there are no Christians there should be Christians.[7]

133

This change in terminology is clearly expressive of a theological shift. Peter Wagner declares: 'The phrase *the church is mission* is more dangerous than it might first appear. It reflects a subtle but widespread shift in emphasis from making disciples as the top priority missionary goal to simply doing good works in the world.'[8]

FROM WHITBY TO UPPSALA

As has been mentioned, Harvey Hoekstra has documented the change which came over missionary thinking. He regards the absorption of the IMC into the WCC and the creation of the CWME as the decisive step in the demise of the IMC and all that it represented. He describes the effect of this re-structuring as follows:

> Formerly it was the IMC and its constituent members who were the experts on the mission of the Church. Now the other divisions within the WCC were giving more time and thought to what mission entailed. The logic was clear enough. If the whole Church was mission . . . (which was what re-interpretation of the term meant), then every division of the WCC was competent to help discover what that mission was. So instead of the CWME infusing the WCC with vision and passion for the unfinished missionary and evangelistic task, other divisions were slowly but steadily shaping the CWME to their concept of mission.[9]

The IMC meeting at Whitby in 1947 was the last occasion on which the 'old' call to fervent and expectant worldwide evangelism was sounded. Five years later at Willingen in West Germany, a different note was audible. There was uncertainty about what constituted mission, what was the place of the church in it and the relation between the church and the kingdom. Yet the Willingen statement still sounded right, because it used classical, biblical language. But that was soon to change. Hoekstra writes:

> No one reading the Willingen documents would have predicted what would be said about mission at Uppsala, only sixteen short years later . . .
>
> In comparing language, style and content of the Willingen documents with statements made by spokesmen of WCC member churches in the seventies, one finds the entire concept of mission changed. Words have been redefined and used in new combinations.[10]

134

What had taken place, then, between Willingen and the 1968 assembly of the WCC at Uppsala in Sweden? In Mexico City in 1963 the CWME held its first meeting since its constitution. It was this meeting which paved the way for Uppsala's enthronement of the 'New Mission'. At Mexico City matters were raised which have been on CWME's agenda ever since. These included:

— *dialogue with people of other living faiths and ideologies;*
— *the relation of dialogue to proclamation and conversion;*
— *the proclamation of the gospel and the social dimension of the gospel;*
— *secular man and the kind of salvation God intends.*

There was one issue which was bigger than all of these and basic to them. R.K. Orchard describes it as follows:

> The discussion raised a theological issue which remained unresolved. Debate returned again and again to the relationship between God's action in and through the Church and everything God is doing in the world apparently independently of the Christian community. Can a distinction be drawn between God's providential action and God's redeeming action?[11]

That such a question should be raised shows how seemingly impregnable theological distinctions can be breached and how the consequences of failing to uphold such distinctions can be ignored.

Between Mexico City and Uppsala another conference was held. This was the World Conference on Church and Society, and it was convened at Geneva in 1966. This aimed to take an entirely new look at the church and her task in a changed world. Involved in the conference were people from various professions, and some were known for their Marxist views of religion, society and economics. Around this time Philip Potter became the director of CWME and he increasingly adopted the WCC views on mission.

The effect of all this was to be seen the following year in the publication of a statement entitled *The Church for Others*. This was produced by the WCC's Department of Studies in Evangelism, which had worked on the Mexico City statement (particularly the relationship between providence and redemption). This working group turned away from thinking of mission as from God, through the church, to the world. Instead, it

135

regarded God's relationship to the world as being direct and primary and sought to fit the church into that scheme. In consequence, it declared:

> We have lifted up humanization as the goal of mission because we believe that more than other positions it communicates in our period of history the meaning of the messianic goal. In another time the goal of God's redemptive work might best have been described in terms of man turning towards God . . . the fundamental question was that of the true God, and the Church responded to that question by pointing to Him. It was *assuming* that the purpose of mission was Christianization, bringing man to God through Christ and His Church. Today the fundamental question is much more that of true man, and the dominant concern of the missionary congregation must therefore be to point to the humanity in Christ as the goal of mission [italics mine].[12]

All this was circulated in preparation for Uppsala and the statement was endorsed there. It was presented at the Assembly by the WCC General Secretary, Dr Eugene Carson Blake, who described the ideas put forward in the statement in terms of renewal of something which had been forgotten rather than as a distortion of the Christian gospel. But his predecessor, Dr Visser 't Hooft declared:

> There is a great tension between the vertical interpretation of the Gospel as essentially concerned with God's saving action in the life of individuals and the horizontal interpretation of it as mainly concerned with human relationships in the world. A Christianity that has lost its vertical dimension has lost its salt, and is not only insipid but useless for the world . . .[13]

He then went on to add a complementary reference to the importance of the horizontal dimension, but his main message was directed against the losing of the vertical. This warning went unheeded and Uppsala approved 'New Mission'.

THE FRANKFURT DECLARATION

The Frankfurt Declaration was issued in March 1970. It was drawn up largely as a result of the concern and work of Dr Peter Beyerhaus, Director of the Institute of the Discipline of Missions and Ecumenical Theology at Tübingen University. It was subscribed by many professors of theology in German universities. Its purpose was to challenge 'the assumptions undergird-

ing the Uppsala Assembly of the World Council of Churches'
and to seek 'to point to the right direction for the mission of the
Church.'[14]

This statement lists *'Seven Indispensable Basic Elements of
Mission'*. In the light of each element, the statement specifies
denials and rejections that relate to that element. Because these
seven principles give an indication of the complexion of
ecumenical theology in 1970, we shall try to summarize them.
We shall then quote important sections of the denial passages
which follow each element mentioned.

1. Matthew 28:18-20 roots mission in the gospel of Christ as
   recorded in the New Testament. After making this point, the
   Declaration continues:

   > *We therefore oppose* the current tendency to determine the nature
   > and task of mission by socio-political analyses of our time and
   > from the demands of the non-Christian world.[15]

2. Ezekiel 38:23 and Romans 15:9 declare that the goal of mission is the glory of the one God and the lordship of His Son.
   In the light of this, the authors of the Declaration state:

   > *We . . . oppose* the assertion that mission today is no longer so
   > concerned with the disclosure of God as with the manifestation of
   > a new man and the extension of a new humanity into all social
   > realms.[16]

3. Acts 4:12 declares the exclusiveness of Christ as Saviour. The
   conclusions which the authors draw from this include the
   following:

   > *We therefore oppose* the false teaching (which has circulated in
   > the ecumenical movement since the Third General Assembly of
   > the World Council of Churches in New Delhi) that Christ Himself
   > is anonymously so evident in world religions, historical changes,
   > and revolutions that man can encounter Him and find salvation in
   > Him without the direct news of the Gospel . . .
   >
   > We likewise reject the unbiblical limitation of the person and
   > work of Jesus to His humanity and ethical example.[17]

4. On the basis of John 3:16 and 2 Corinthians 5:20, which
   speak of individual belief and repentance and the danger of
   damnation, the statement declares:

   > *We . . . oppose* the universalistic idea that in the crucifixion and
   > resurrection of Jesus Christ all men of all times are already born

137

again and already have peace with Him, irrespective of their knowledge of the historical saving activity of God or belief in it.[18]

5. 1 Peter 2:9 and Romans 12:2 declare that the task of mission is to call out a community for the Lord from all peoples. The authors therefore state:

> *We . . . oppose* the view that the Church . . . is simply a part of the world. The contrast between the Church and the world is not merely a distinction in function . . . rather, it is an essential difference in nature. We deny that the Church has no advantage over the world except the knowledge of the alleged future salvation of all men.
>
> We further oppose the one-sided emphasis on salvation which stresses only this world, according to which the Church and the world together share in a future, purely social, reconciliation of all mankind.[19]

6. Ephesians 2:11-12 describes how salvation has been extended to Gentiles as well as Jews. Therefore:

> We . . . reject the false teaching that non-Christian religions . . . are also ways of salvation similar to belief in Christ.
>
> We refute the idea that 'Christian presence' among the adherents to world religions and a give-and-take dialogue with them are substitutes for a proclamation of the Gospel which aims at conversion. Such dialogues simply establish good points of contact for missionary communication.
>
> We also refute the claim that the borrowing of Christian ideas, hopes and social procedures . . . can make world religions and ideologies substitutes for the Church of Jesus Christ. In reality they give them a syncretistic and therefore anti-Christian direction.[20]

7. Matthew 24:14 declares: '. . . and then the end will come' (RSV). Christian mission is a preparation for that. Since that is the case, the statement continues:

> *We refute* the unfounded idea that the eschatological expectation of the New Testament has been falsified by Christ's delay in returning and is therefore to be given up . . .
>
> We refute the identification of messianic salvation with progress, development, and social change. The fatal consequence of this is that efforts to aid development and revolutionary involvement in the places of tension in society are seen as the contemporary forms of Christian mission.[21]

These negations give an accurate picture of how mission was

regarded in ecumenical circles at that time. Coming as they do from Dr Beyerhaus, these denials and refutations cannot be lightly dismissed. Like Hoekstra, he is actively involved in the development of missionary thought within such circles. In addition, these denials describe in part the challenge which LCWE and WEF have to face in their missiological studies.

Bangkok (1973)

Three years after the publication of the Frankfurt Declaration, the WCC held its assembly in Bangkok. This 1973 conference went further down the same road as Uppsala. The theme was 'Salvation Today'. This was defined as having four components: economic, political, social, and personal salvation. All the time was given to the first three elements. Bangkok dismissed the Frankfurt Declaration.

THEOLOGICAL INFLUENCES

One man who has been particularly influential in the emergence and development of this theology of 'New Mission' is J.C. Hoekendijk. He came from a family committed to the Dutch pentecostal movement. From 1957 to his death in 1974 he bitterly opposed what he called the 'church-centredness' of the 'old' missionary enterprise — that is, mission being to the world through the church and with a view to planting churches. He was active at Willingen in 1952 and subsequently.

The idea that God dealt with the world through the church in any sense was obnoxious to him. The pattern God-world-church instead of God-church-world represents his thinking. Mission was the mission of God (*Missio Dei*) and not the mission of the church, let alone the missions of the churches. The *Missio Dei* is God's activity in the world process, His work of liberating, renewing, and bringing about the kingdom — a universal shalom. 'The Church for others' was his term for a church which denied its distinctiveness and submerged its conscious identity in this ongoing process. Harvey Cox gave the name 'humanization' to this process and aim.

Coupled with this theology of secularization (for that is its aim) is another ingredient. It is the theology of dialogue. Dietrich Bonhoeffer's views of the desacralization of the world and religionless society were very influential here. 'Dialogue' no longer means a serious and open-ended discussion between the varying Christian traditions alone. The world and mankind are bigger than the churches, and so ideologies and religions other than Christian ones must also be included. A united world society cannot be achieved only by a united church active in the face of deprivation and dehumanization — there must be a link between Christianity and the other (and older) religions of the world. Underlying and uniting Christian trinitarianism and the gods of the nations, so the argument goes, is a common monism. A cosmic Christ unites Jesus of Nazareth and other religious prophets and leaders, and a world spirit replaces the Holy Spirit of God and Christ.

Hoekstra sums up the features of the scene as follows:

> The new perspectives which shaped the quest for a reconceptualization of mission owe as much to ideology as theology. The secular became sacred and the sacred became secular. In speaking of man one somehow spoke of God. Man became all important. 'Doing theology' became fashionable; one acted first and thought about its significance later. Action/reflection was how one came to understand what God was doing and the manner in which one joined him. Propositional statements about God, the Church, and the world were eschewed. Third World Christians were warned about theologies that suited the Western-oriented view of reality. Instead, experience should be their criteria; one compared experiences to know what God was doing and what was real. Wide varieties of religious or liberating experiences were shared to illustrate the variety of ways in which God's salvation was provided. Proof texts from the Scriptures were cited to confirm assumptions actually based elsewhere.[22]

*   *   *   *   *

MISSION AND EVANGELISM: AN APPRAISAL

Now that we have set *M & E* in its historical and theological context, we can now proceed to look at its contents. We shall make a selection of subjects in the light of the following facts.

Uppsala and Bangkok represent the high water mark of 'New Mission'. At the Fifth General Assembly of the WCC in Nairobi, protests were raised and that view of mission was challenged from both the floor and the platform. Bishop Arias and Rev. John Stott opposed the trend. What would the WCC and CWME make of this? *M & E* is the result of a request which was made following the Nairobi meeting. How does *M & E* relate to 'New Mission'? Does it reject it or not? Has the Frankfurt Declaration now been heeded? The answer is not easy to give and is probably yes *and* no. To see if we can arrive at a clearer answer, we shall look at what *M & E* has to say about the gospel, conversion, and particularly about witness to other religions.

THE GOSPEL ITSELF

Nowhere in this document is there anything approaching a definition of the gospel. In this respect *M & E* stands in marked contrast to *BEM*, in which there are definitions of both baptism and eucharist. This omission is important, because lack of precision about what constitutes the gospel is bound to lead to confused thinking and acting with respect to mission and evangelism. We ought to note in passing that even with its clear emphasis on the greatness of the gospel, the New Testament does contain definitions of what the gospel is. 1 Corinthians 15:1-4 is an example of this.

However, *M & E* does supply a description of what the gospel brings and does. As this is the case, the absence of even a working definition may be regarded by some as no great loss. Still, such a definition would have been helpful, because a definition summarizes the essential features of something in contradistinction to everything else. It is part of *M & E*'s weakness that it does not state precisely what its view of the gospel is and what it is not. But ecumenical statements are not renowned for such precision.

The horizontal and the vertical

A certain framework is nevertheless discernible in what *M & E* says about the gospel. It is heavily orientated towards kingdom theology. Indeed, it is not too much to say that this perspective predominates. There can be no objection to the good news being described as 'the kingdom of God inaugurated in Jesus the Lord, crucified and risen'.[23] The New Testament so describes it. Jesus spoke of it in this way (Mark 1:15) and so did Paul (Acts 28:23). There is no problem with the terminology itself; the problem concerns its meaning. *What is the kingdom?* R.T. France describes the term *kingdom* as a 'hurray-word' in theological circles[24] — one which rings all sorts of bells and creates all sorts of 'vibes'. In the New Testament the kingdom is a very large subject and one which cannot be examined in any detail here. We can say, however, that the primary meaning of 'kingdom' is 'reign' and not 'realm'. As a result, the question which must be faced is not, 'What or where is the kingdom?', but, 'How does God reign in the world through Jesus Christ?'

To that question *M & E* replies that He does so *predominantly* in a socio-political way. This is a personal judgment and therefore one which must be supported. If this view is correct, then Uppsala and Bangkok have not been totally endorsed. At the same time, it is equally true to say that they have not been totally rejected either. The all-important question is, 'Has the balance been redressed sufficiently to enable the gospel to be regarded as *primarily* spiritual — not physical, heavenly and eschatological, or earthly and temporal?' On the basis of Visser 't Hooft's terms, the answer to that must be no. *M & E* is *more* horizontal than vertical.

Man's sin and guilt before God

This can be seen in the way that *M & E* treats sin. The preface declares:

> Sin, alienating persons from God, neighbour and nature, is found both in individual and corporate forms, both in slavery of the human will and in social, political and economic structures of domination and dependence.[25]

While this excerpt does speak of alienation and bondage (the vertical dimension), it will be noticed that sin's presence in others and its effects upon them on the horizontal plane are put on a par with that. In addition, more is said about the latter than about the former. This is typical of the rest of the statement. It expatiates on man's inhumanity to man and brings this to a focus in the case of the poor. These are the ones who are sinned against. At times one even wonders whether they are sinless and therefore in a position to merit the gospel! This is certainly 'horizontal thinking'.

But what of the allusions to alienation from God and bondage to sin? Even these are not as vertical in their reference as the New Testament is when it speaks of sin. Alienation and bondage speak of sin's effect on the sinner. Alienation describes what he lacks, while bondage describes what has overcome him. Although the former of these terms does bring God into the

142

equation, neither of them describes sin's effect on *God*, but only on man. Both words may therefore still be termed 'horizontal'.

There is, however, one occasion, and only one, when the word 'guilt' appears. Yet it is not explained, and it could mean no more than a feeling of guilt. The relevant sentence is: 'Christ's identification with humanity went even more deeply, and while nailed on the cross accused as a political criminal, he took upon himself the guilt even of those who crucified him.'[26] Even if this be regarded as referring to a state of being guilty before God, it is restricted only to his crucifiers.

The significant omission in *M & E*'s references to sin is the absence of any statement about what sin means to God. There is nothing about what effect sin has on Him and what His reaction is to it. There is no reference to sin's offensiveness to a holy and righteous God, and no hint of the culpability of those who practise it. *M & E* is therefore not fully vertical, even when it speaks of God. It is predominantly horizontal.

The nature of the gospel

This same deficiency can be seen in what *M & E* says about the gospel. So prominent does the socio-political element become that the gospel cannot be made known without it. The statement declares: 'Proclamation that does not hold forth the promises of the justice of the kingdom to the poor of the earth is a caricature of the Gospel.' Underlying that claim is the following view: 'The "spiritual gospel" and "material gospel" were in Jesus one Gospel.' [27]

This theology is based on a particular understanding of the Gospels and the kingdom. While it does not exclude the spiritual element (which would have been the effect of Uppsala and Bangkok), it does oppose its being regarded as the exclusive element or even the primary element. This is the area in which liberation theology operates. Evangelical theology, on the other hand, faces a major difficulty here, because it is divided on the subject. Evangelicals have yet to resolve the question: 'Is the gospel of the kingdom primarily and initially spiritual, and *then* social through churches or individual Christians, or, is it *as much* social as spiritual (and vice versa)?' The spectre of a 'new' social gospel certainly looms among evangelicals.[28]

There can be no doubt that the primary-secondary distinction is rejected by *M & E*. The authors of the document make it plain that, in their view, the gospel has as much to do with social, technological, biological, industrial, economic and political factors as spiritual ones. These are by necessary implication identified with the 'principalities and powers' of the New Testament. The demonic and satanic realm is alien to this document, and perhaps anathema. Here is another instance of *M & E*'s horizontal nature. Though the gospel is an expression of God's great love, it is a 'new justice', a 'change from war to peace, from injustice, from racism to solidarity, from hate to love.'[29]

The death of Christ

Similarly, when the Godward side of the gospel is considered, there is a failure to do justice to the New Testament teaching. This is especially the case with regard to the death of Christ. *M & E* refers to the fact of Christ's death and mentions that it was by crucifixion. In addition, the term 'self-surrendering' and the expression 'gave his own life' are used to describe Christ's voluntary action in dying.[30] In relation to God, Christ's death is seen as an expression of His great love to the world. But all this is connected with the movement of the gospel towards *man*. What about the reverse dimension? Did Christ do anything on the cross with reference to *God*?

The document says that 'he took our predicament on the cross'.[31] But this is vague and probably means no more than *M & E*'s earlier declaration that 'misery, sin and death are defeated'.[32] Similarly, the statement already quoted about 'guilt' is not explained. This is surprising, because 2 Corinthians 5:21 is quoted later, but again without any comment. Though the imagery of 'a sacrificed lamb' is quoted, it is not interpreted — as it ought to be — against the sacrificial background of the Old Testament, but rather in terms of the reigning Lamb of the Book of Revelation.[33] But the Lamb who reigns is the Lamb who died, and He reigns only because He died. In His death He offered Himself to God as both priest and sacrifice, and that sacrifice was for sin. However, all notion of propitiating God is alien to this document, in which sin does not merit punishment, and God is not a God of wrath. Any notion of eternal punishment is regarded as impossible. The only conflict which took place on the cross was between 'the powers of evil and the love of God'.[34]

The consequence of all this is that what is said about the

gospel (i.e. human sin and divine salvation) lacks that fully vertical element which is found in the New Testament and which constitutes the heart, the *sine qua non*, of the Christian doctrine of the atonement. This is a serious omission. It produces a man-centred view of salvation. This statement about the gospel is not free from the weaknesses of Uppsala and Bangkok.

CONVERSION

In what *M & E* says about conversion the same conjunction of elements is noticeable as was discovered in relation to the gospel — that is, the horizontal and the vertical. Here again, Uppsala is neither completely renounced nor completely endorsed. Furthermore, the horizontal dimension carries the greater weight.

The necessity of conversion is something which has to be *deduced* from *M & E*, because there is no unambiguous statement about it in the document. We find that conversion is equated with regeneration, and that the Holy Spirit's role in this 'conversion' is to *help* the offer of fellowship to be accepted. Furthermore, conversion is regarded as an ongoing process. Its initial, once-for-all nature (cf. justification in chapter 3) is rejected. The document borrows the following definition of conversion from the report of a consultation of Orthodox theologians:

> [Conversion is] *from* a life characterized by sin, separation from God, submission to evil and the unfulfilled potential of God's image, *to* a new life characterized by the forgiveness of sins, obedience to the commands of God, renewed fellowship with God in Trinity, growth in the restoration of the divine image and the realization . . . of the love of Christ.[35]

While this statement does have the appearance of stressing the vertical dimension, to which we have already referred, we must point out that sin's effect on God and His wrath against sinners are not mentioned. The statement is therefore not as fully vertical as the New Testament is. In addition, it is found side by side with other statements about conversion which give priority to the horizontal (the social dimension). In paragraph 11 we find the following statement:

> While the basic experience of conversion is the same, the awareness of an encounter with God revealed in Christ, the concrete occasion of this experience and the actual shape of the same differs in terms of our personal situation.[36]

This statement is then explained by references to what John the Baptist told the soldiers to do and to what Jesus told the rich young ruler to do. Yet, in both of these incidents from the Gospels, the reference was to a test of true conversion, and not to something which is part and parcel of it. Later on, in paragraph 14 of *M & E*, the priority of the horizontal is taken up again and explicitly stated. The relevant sentence is:

> 'If salvation from sin through divine forgiveness is to be truly and fully personal, it must express itself in the renewal of these relations and structures [i.e. of society]. Such renewal is not merely a consequence, but *an essential element* of the conversion of whole human beings' [italics mine].[37]

This must mean that those who repent of their sins, trust in God's mercy through the atoning death of Christ and yield themselves to God for His service are not really converted, unless they also adopt an antagonistic stance to social injustice and act accordingly. Is this conversion as the Bible presents it? Evidence is not the same as essence. Fruit is not identical with root. This is to give the horizontal pre-eminence over the vertical, and the physical priority over the spiritual.

WITNESS

Social critique

We have noted *M & E*'s insistence that the proclamation of the gospel must include a social critique or else become a caricature of the gospel. The document uses a very strong expression to make this point, and we can see it in the following extract: 'The church is called *to announce* Good News in Jesus Christ, forgiveness, hope, a new heaven and a new earth; *to denounce* powers and principalities, sin and injustice.'[38]

This element of denunciation stands out in *M & E* and, for that matter, in other ecumenical documents. It is hard to think of a parallel instance because, generally speaking, negations are not that plentiful, let alone denunciations. Yet, in this single context — the proclamation of the gospel — denunciation of wickedness in social systems is essential to its authentic communication. Support for this is derived from the ministry of the prophets in the Old Testament and from Jesus' censures of the rich and powerful in the New. But did not the prophets and

Jesus speak *just as strongly* against false religion and false teachers, that is, against idolatry and heterodoxy? Did they not denounce man-made traditions?

Other religions

When we look at the section of *M & E* devoted to witnessing to believers in other religions, that note of strong criticism is completely absent. Indeed, the title of this section is not without significance. It is 'Witness among people of living faiths'. This seems to say more about non-Christian religions than it does about those who believe in them. It would not be right to dismiss the sincerity of such people, but one can refrain from doing that without giving the least sign that their religious systems are valid and acceptable before God.

M & E declares that the Word and the Spirit are present and active not only in individuals, but also in non-Christian religions and ideologies. It affirms:

> The Word is at work in every human life . . . The Spirit of God is constantly at work in ways that pass human understanding and in places that to us are least expected. In entering into a relationship of dialogue with others, therefore, Christians seek to discern the unsearchable riches of God and the way he deals with humanity.[39]

This kind of thinking is the product of faulty exegesis. John 1 distinguishes between the creative and providential work of the Logos on the one hand, and His redemptive work on the other. To fail to do so is the result of erasing the distinction (to which we referred earlier on) between providence and redemption.

This kind of approach to other religions is what lay behind the thinking of Archbishop Runcie in his lecture entitled 'Christianity and World Religions'. There he stated that 'other faiths than our own are genuine mansions of the Spirit'[40] and that they have 'movements of revelation and . . . spiritual treasures'[41] to share with Christians.

After expressing his gratitude that such dialogue enables people 'to avoid making crude choices between what is "true" and what is "false" in different religions', the archbishop declares:

> I am reminded of a story told by Ninian Smart of the lady missionary who was driving him to a hospital not far from Benares. They passed a shrine, and she remarked: 'I'm always very sad to

see the piety with which those Hindus worship at that shrine'. He asked why. 'Well', she said with a sort of simple finality, 'there's no one there to hear them'.

The archbishop then added:

> That 'simple finality' has no place today. Was it Max Muller who urged that in respect of religion 'He who knows one, knows none'?[42]

Although the Bible does declare the immensity of the one God, it also asserts the deceptiveness of idols (Ps. 115). If any connection is made between idols and the supernatural, it is made with demons and not God (1 Cor. 10:21-22).

While *M & E* declares that 'Christians owe the message of God's salvation in Jesus Christ to every person and to every people' and that 'in Him is *our* salvation' (i.e. the salvation of Christians), it does not say that all need that message and that there is no salvation in anyone else but in Jesus Christ. *M & E* states: 'Among Christians there are still differences of understanding as to how this salvation in Christ is available to people of diverse religious persuasions.'[43] This is to deny that for 'every creature . . . under heaven' (Col.1:23) faith in Christ alone is the necessary condition of salvation. The Frankfurt Declaration has not been heeded.

This uncertainty about the way salvation is available to non-Christians is tantamount to denying both the exclusiveness of the Christian gospel and its universal authority and relevance. This can be seen in what *M & E* says about witnessing. It directs the cutting edge of its statements on this subject more towards Christians than non-Christians. It declares:

> True witness follows Jesus Christ in respecting and affirming the uniqueness and freedom of others . . . we have often looked for the worst in others and have passed negative judgement upon other religions . . . Witness cannot be a one-way process, but of necessity is two-way; in it Christians become aware of some of the deepest convictions of their neighbours.[44]

This is what is meant by 'a relationship of dialogue'. It is regarded as taking place in a multi-religious situation, and there can be no doubt that it does create problems for witnessing. Adherents of non-Christian religions are sensitive on this point, and so is the WCC. It has moved from declaring a kind of moratorium on proselytizing to actually favouring the validity of non-Christian religions. This has an effect not only on the gospel but also on the church. At the WCC assembly in Nairobi, the song which expressed this thinking was: 'Break down the walls which divide us and unite us in one body'. This was not a reference to the divisions between the churches alone. It was the 'pop' answer to the following question which that assembly was called to consider: 'The church is called to be there for others. What should we contribute therefore to the construction of a larger community which God in Christ has in mind for men of all religions, cultures and ideologies?'[45]

The motto of the Ecumenical Movement used to be derived from John 17:22. It was: 'That they all may be one'. The unity envisaged by this statement concerned the various branches of the church. As a result, *inter-confessional* dialogue was pursued to resolve the disagreements between them. But it is no longer a 'Coming World Church' which the WCC has in view. It is rather a 'Coming World Humanity' or a 'Coming World Community'. A different text (Eph. 1:10) has therefore been borrowed to convey this perception. From an exegetical point of view, this text has been more abused than John 17:22, because the gathering together of everything in Christ is construed to mean not merely the church, but also a multi-religious community on earth. According to this interpretation, Christ is to be regarded as a cosmic figure who is present in a hidden way in all religions. The conclusion to which this view leads its proponents is that *inter-faith* dialogue must take place.

Stanley J. Samartha was the Director of the WCC Unit on Dialogue with People of Living Faiths and Ideologies. He still exerts an influence on WCC thinking on this subject. Following Nairobi, he described the role of the WCC as being partly that of an 'enabler or partner in dialogues with people of various faiths and ideologies' and as 'a catalyst in ecumenical thinking and action for theological reflections and for practical co-operation together with people of other faiths and ideologies'.[46]

As an example of such co-operation, we can refer to the day of prayer which was held in Assisi on 27 October 1986, when leaders of all the main world religions joined the Pope in prayer for peace. Archbishop Runcie, Cardinal Hume and leaders of the Jewish, Muslim, Hindu, Buddhist, Sikh and Shinto faiths were present. Peace was one of the subjects which Samartha had urged those involved in inter-faith dialogue to consider. Other suitable topics were: 'spirituality, poverty, science and technology, the status and role of women, power and land'[47] — hardly the distinctives of Christianity!

Since the Nairobi Assembly, the WCC has given a considerable amount of thought to the subject of dialogue. In 1977 it sponsored a Theological Consultation on 'Dialogue in Community'. This was held at Chiang Mai in Thailand. The topic was also discussed at the Sixth Assembly of the World Council of Churches in Vancouver. An inherent tension is evident in the statements which were issued by both of these gatherings. In our opinion, it amounts to a standing contradiction. On the one hand, the truth of the gospel of Christ is acknowledged; yet, on the other hand, redemptive truth is said to be present in non-Christian religions. This means that Christ is found in non-Christian religions and that those who practise them witness to Him. To try to speak of witness in the New Testament sense *and* to engage in dialogue in the ecumenical sense is an impossibility. The Vancouver report declares: 'Dialogue is not a device for nor a denial of Christian witness. It is rather a mutual venture to bear witness to each other and the world in relation to different perceptions of ultimate reality.'[48]

Long ago, Visser 't Hooft, the first General Secretary of the WCC, warned against 'the view that there is no unique revelation in history, that there are many different ways to reach the divine reality, that all formulations of religious truth or experience are by their very nature inadequate expressions of the truth and that it is necessary to harmonize as much as possible all religious ideas and experiences so as to create one universal religion for mankind.'[49]

Conclusion

For all the attempt which the WCC makes to assert the Christian message, the presence of the social (and even the political) dimension in its thinking, coupled with the pluralism of its religious outlook, undermine that message and will eventually eradicate it. Taken separately, the social dimension and the multi-religious outlook are serious enough from the standpoint of the biblical gospel. Taken together, they are fatal, because whatever scholars and theological experts may say, ordinary people will be given to understand that this life is at least as important as the next, and that there are many ways to heaven, whatever it may be like.

Postscript

In examining ecumenism our main purpose has been to discover what bearing it has on the biblical gospel and evangelicalism, and what its consequences are for them. In these final pages we shall try to show what conclusions are to be drawn from this, as far as evangelicals are concerned. We shall then seek to lay a challenge before them.

The adjective 'ecumenical' is not found in any English translation of the Scriptures, but the noun *oikoumene* (the 'logo' of the WCC) occurs several times in the New Testament. *Oikoumene* means the 'inhabited earth or world'. We shall survey and categorize the uses of the word in order to draw together the threads of our study.

First of all, there are a number of verses in which the term *oikoumene* is used to refer to the Roman Empire, because, in the thinking of the time, the Empire was identical with the populated world. These verses are to be found in the Book of Acts (e.g. 17:6; 19:27; 24:5). We should also include in this category Luke 2:1, where we read in the King James Version that 'all the *world* should be taxed'.

Secondly, a number of texts, which contain the word, use it to make a connection between the populated world and the salvation provided by the gospel. In Hebrews 1:6 the *oikoumene* is the realm into which the Son of God came. In Matthew 24:14 and Romans 10:18 it is to the *oikoumene* that the gospel is to be preached. This is set against the back-cloth of the judgments of God on the *oikoumene* because of human sin. These will culminate in the judgment of the Last Day (Luke 21:26; Acts 11:28, 17:31; Rev. 3:10).

Thirdly, Satan is active in relation to the *oikoumene*. It was

153

'all the kingdoms of the world' that Satan displayed and offered Jesus in the temptation (Luke 4:5). In Revelation 12:9 the entire *oikoumene* is described as being deceived by Satan. In Revelation 16:14 the kings of the whole *oikoumene*, duped and motivated by Satan and his minions, all gathered together for 'battle on the great day of God the Almighty' (RSV).

We can draw two conclusions from all this with regard to our study and its purpose:

1. The use of the term 'ecumenical' in the WCC context is not a biblical one. The New Testament does not use *oikoumene* to refer to the church, but rather to refer to the world. This fact is not in itself sufficient to establish the case that the Ecumenical Movement is unbiblical, but it should be enough to make us pause at least before endorsing the WCC as biblically valid.

2. The crucial questions to be decided are not, of course, matters of terminology but of theology. We must first ask whether what is described as 'ecumenical' is consonant with Scripture. One could, for example, describe the love of God as ecumenical because of what John 3:16 declares about it. However, the term 'cosmos' in that verse is used to make clear that God loves a fallen race, and not just people scattered over the globe. Similarly, one could speak of sin and judgment as being ecumenical, because the New Testament declares them to be world-wide. Yet the real question here is, *'Can the term be used in a biblical sense with regard to the Church of the WCC?'*

In our view, that question must be answered negatively. The 'Coming World Church' of ecumenism is *not* the church which is delineated in the New Testament. Since that is the case, the movement attached to the term is unbiblical.

But is the adjective 'ecumenical' wholly devoid of any biblical support when used in connection with the WCC? According to our second category of usage (see above), it certainly is. The Ecumenical Movement is not in keeping with the gospel. But there is a third category of usage. What is ecumenical in the New Testament does not have to be *evangelical* to be ecumenical. It can be *Satanic* and ecumenical. This can even apply to something religious, because the New Testament tells us that Satan not only rules over a kingdom which is social in its manifestation (Eph. 2:1-3), but one which can even take ecclesiastical form and shape (2 Thess. 2). The man of sin 'sits as

God in the temple of God, showing himself that he is God' (2 Thess. 2:4 RAV).

The big question, therefore, is: 'What kind of ecumenism does the WCC present and practice?' Is it of God or of Satan? Is it of Christ or of antichrist? The answer to these questions is determined by the answer to another, namely: 'Is it expressive of and in keeping with the gospel or not?' Ecumenism has to be evangelical, otherwise it is Satanic.

We have tried to show how the ecumenism of the WCC is not in keeping with the gospel. It is not based on an infallible Scripture, but allows for an open canon and for the development of tradition in and by, the church. This undermines authority. In addition, it does not confess that Christ's work on the cross is so acceptable to the Father that any notion of its being repeated or re-presented denies the atonement. It refuses to say that faith without works is the *only* way by which Christ and His salvation may be received by the ungodly, but asserts instead that it *may* be so received. To do that is to deny the heart of the good news and to deprive the sinner of any assurance of eternal life. Authority, atonement, acceptance with God, assurance — all are countered in WCC theology. Instead, one is left with a sacramental and sacerdotal community, where socializing has become the primary effect. This ecumenism has all the appearances of being Satanic in origin, character and aim. Bishop Spong of Newark, New Jersey, described in the following words what must logically be the way to WCC unity:

> If Christian unity is to be achieved, Christian pluralism will have to be affirmed and the relativity of all Christian truth will have to be established. This reality makes us aware that every narrow definition of Christian doctrinal certainty will finally have to be abandoned; every claim by any branch of the Christian church to be the true church or the only church will ultimately have to be sacrificed; every doctrine of infallibility — whether of the papacy, or of the Scriptures, or of any sacred tradition, or of any individual experience — will inevitably have to be forgotten.[1]

It is therefore not logically possible to be for the biblical gospel *and* for WCC ecumenism. This does not mean that no Christians are to be found in WCC-aligned churches, or anything so crass. But it does mean that all who are for the gospel should be openly against WCC ecumenism. The gospel necessitates that stance.

155

But the gospel also necessitates another stance. Jesus rejected Satan's ecumenical community to create one of His own. He came to earth to die not only for Jews but to gather together into one the children of God who were scattered abroad (John 11:52). This is an ecumenism which the gospel creates. It is an ecumenism which in turn commends the gospel. For evangelicals to reject a false ecumenism opposed to the gospel in which they believe, and yet to fail to embrace and pursue the ecumenism created by the selfsame gospel is horrid and hypocritical. 'These things ought not so to be' (Jas. 3:10). Evangelical ecumenism cannot be restricted to private fellowship on the one hand or parachurch organizations on the other. It must involve the churches and inter-church life and witness, because God sent His Son into the world to live and die for a church. A single gospel and a disunited church is a standing contradiction.

Unity is not the same as union. Unity is an attitude and a relationship between persons, and not primarily a structure or a form. It is therefore compatible with a rich diversity and even with disagreements.

But to pursue unity means that we must have a sense of proportion with regard to our disagreements. This perspective is derived from the subject about which we are agreed, namely, what constitutes the gospel. Those things about which we are in disagreement do not destroy those beliefs which we hold in common. That means that one set of truths is more important than the other. God makes this distinction among mankind, and so it is not improper for us to make it. What is more, unless we do so, we shall never have unity. We must, therefore, not allow our conscientiously held beliefs about baptism, church government, baptism with the Spirit and charismatic gifts, prophecy and the millennium, Bible translations and so on to curtail our unity and to hinder its growth between our churches. This is no *easy* path to tread, but Romans 14 and 15 show the way forward. In the church at Rome disagreements existed as to whether or not Old Testament regulations about days and food still provided Christians with a framework for their service to the Lord. There were two groups in that church: one was theologically right and the other wrong, but both were spiritually wrong. Righteousness, peace and joy in the Holy Spirit were common to both and to be recognized in each. On that basis they were to 'pursue the things which make for peace and the things by which one may edify another' (Rom. 14:19 RAV). So must we. On the other hand, however, they were all to 'note those who cause divisions' contrary to the doctrine they had learned and to avoid them (Rom. 16:17 RAV). We must do that too.

References

Chapter 1. Scripture and Tradition

1. *The Fourth World Conference on Faith and Order, Montreal 1963*, edited by P.C. Rodger and L. Vischer, Faith and Order Paper, no. 42 (SCM Press, 1964), pp.50-61.
2. See *The Bible: its Authority and Interpretation in the Ecumenical Movement*, edited by Ellen Flesseman-van Leer, Faith and Order Paper, no. 99 (WCC, 1983).
3. Ibid., p.viii.
4. Quoted in B. Till, *The Churches Search for Unity* (Penguin, 1972), p.239.
5. *Faith and Order Findings*, edited by Paul S. Minear, Faith and Order Paper, no. 40 (SCM, 1963), p.10.
6. Ibid., p.15.
7. Rodger and Vischer, op. cit., p.51.
8. Y.M. Congar, *Tradition and Traditions* (Burns & Oates, 1966).
9. *The Documents of Vatican II*, edited by W.M. Abbott and J. Gallagher (Geoffrey Chapman, 1966).
10. Xavier Rynne, *Letters from Vatican City* (Faber, 1963), p.143.
11. *Holy Book and Holy Tradition*, edited by E.G. Rupp and F.F. Bruce (Manchester University Press, 1968), pp.155-56.
12. See *The Teaching of the Catholic Church*, edited by Karl Rahner (Mercier Press, 1967). Originally prepared by J. Neuner and H. Roos.
13. Abbott & Gallagher, op.cit., p.128.
14. Ibid., p.112.
15. B.C. Butler, *The Theology of Vatican II* (Darton, Longman & Todd, 1967).
16. Ibid., p.29.
17. *Commentary on the Documents of Vatican II*, edited by Herbert Vorgrimler, Vol. 3 (Search Press, 1968), p.164.
18. Ibid., p.171.
19. See J. Baillie, *The Idea of Revelation in Recent Thought* (Oxford University Press, 1956). See also:
   Leon Morris, *I Believe in Revelation* (Hodder and Stoughton, 1976).
   H.D. McDonald, *Ideas of Revelation: 1700-1869* (Macmillan, 1959).
   H.D. McDonald, *Theories of Revelation: 1860-1900* (Allen & Unwin, 1963).
20. Butler, op. cit., pp.29-30.

21. Ibid.
22. Ibid.
23. Ibid.
24. Abbott & Gallagher, op. cit., p.114.
25. Ibid., pp.114-15.
26. Ibid., p.117.
27. Ibid., p.115.
28. Ibid., p.117.
29. Ibid.
30. Ibid., p.116.
31. Ibid.
32. Butler, op. cit., p.30.
33. Abbott & Gallagher, op. cit., pp.116-17.
34. Ibid., p.115.
35. Ibid., p.116.
36. Vorgrimler, op. cit., p.183.
37. Abbott & Gallagher, op. cit., p.116.
38. Ibid., p.120.
39. Butler, op. cit., p.44.
40. G.H. Tavard, *Holy Writ or Holy Church* (Burns & Oates, 1959).
41. Rahner, op. cit., p.62.
42. Butler, op. cit., p.46.
43. Rahner, op. cit., p.62.
44. *The New Catholic Encyclopaedia*, Vol. 2 (McGraw-Hill, 1967), p.384.
45. Abbott & Gallagher, op. cit., pp.118-19.
46. See A.R. Vidler, *The Modernist Movement in the Roman Church* (Cambridge University Press, 1934).
47. Abbott & Gallagher, op.cit., p.120.
48. Butler, op. cit., p.53.
49. Rupp and Bruce, op. cit., p.166.
50. See 1 (above).
51. Rodger and Vischer, op. cit., p.50.
52. Ibid., p.51.
53. Rupp and Bruce, op. cit., pp.154-70.
54. Rodger and Vischer, op. cit., p.58.
55. Ibid., p.51.
56. Ibid.
57. Ibid.
58. Ibid., p.50.
59. Ibid.
60. Minear, op. cit., pp.16-17.
61. Quotation taken from Minear, op cit., part 4 (pp.3-63).
62. Rodger and Vischer, op. cit., p.51.
63. Minear, op. cit., p.15.
64. As 61 above.
65. Newspeak was the official language of Oceania in George Orwell's novel *1984*. The language was designed to produce thoughtless conformity with the will of the Party which ruled Oceania.
66. Rodger and Vischer, op. cit., p.24.
67. Ibid., p.25.

68. Ibid., p.52.
69. J.P. Mackey, *The Modern Theology of Tradition* (Darton, Longman & Todd, 1962), p.x.
70. Rodger and Vischer, op. cit., p.52.
71. As 61 above.
72. Ibid., p.17.
73. Rodger and Vischer, op. cit., p.52.
74. See 9 above.
75. Abbott & Gallagher, op. cit., p.132.
76. Rodger and Vischer, op. cit., p.52.
77. Ibid., pp.58-9.
78. Ibid., p.55.
79. Minear, op. cit., pp.13-15.
80. See chapter 3.
81. Rodger and Vischer, op. cit., p.53.
82. *Ecumenical Review*, 23:4 (October 1971), pp.335-46.
83. *Biblical Authority for Today*, edited by A. Richardson and W. Schweitzer (SCM Press, 1951).
84. *New Delhi Speaks*, edited by W.A. Visser 't Hooft (SCM Press, 1962).
85. The new statement is: 'The World Council of Churches is a fellowship of churches which confess the Lord Jesus Christ as God and Saviour according to the Scriptures and therefore seek to fulfil together their common calling to the glory of the one God, Father, Son and Holy Spirit.'
86. Rodger and Vischer, op. cit., p.17. *Heilsgeschichte* is the German term for salvation-history.
87. Flesseman-van Leer, op. cit., p.4.
88. Rodger and Vischer, op. cit., p.54.
89. Ibid.
90. Flesseman-van Leer, op. cit., p.5.
91. See James Barr, 'The Authority of the Bible: a Study Outline', *Ecumenical Review*, 21:2 (April 1969).
92. Flesseman-van Leer, op. cit., p.31.
93. Ibid.
94. Ibid., pp.31-2.
95. Barr, op. cit., p.135.
96. Flesseman-van Leer, op. cit., p.32.
97. Ibid., p.32.
98. Ibid., p.40.
99. Barr, op. cit., p.135.
100. Flesseman-van Leer, op. cit., p.52.
101. Barr, op. cit., p.140.
102. Ibid., p.40.
103. Flesseman-van Leer, op. cit., p.48.
104. Ibid., p.47.
105. Anglican-Roman Catholic International Commission, *The Final Report* (CTS/SPCK, 1982), p.52.
106. Flesseman-van Leer, op. cit., p.48.
107. Ibid., pp.53-4.
108. Ibid., p.54.
109. Ibid., p.48.

Chapter 2. The Death of Christ

1. 1 Timothy 3:15.
2. Anglican-Roman Catholic International Commission, *The Final Report* (CTS/SPCK, 1982), p.11. It is to this document that we refer when we use the designation 'ARCIC' or 'the ARCIC statement' in this and other chapters of this book.
3. Hans Küng, *Infallible?* (Collins, 1971).
4. Hans Küng, *Why Priests?* (Collins, 1972).
5. Ibid., p.43.
6. 'The Constitution on the Sacred Liturgy' in *Vatican Council II: The Conciliar and Post-Conciliar Documents*, edited by Austin Flannery (Dominican Publications, 1980). In this chapter we refer to this publication as 'Vatican II'.
7. Ibid., p.17.
8. Ibid., p.18.
9. See *The Teaching of the Catholic Church*, edited by Karl Rahner (Mercier Press, 1967). Originally prepared by J. Neuner and H. Roos. This is a translation of a selection from Denzinger's *Enchiridion*.
10. Quoted in David N. Samuel, *Pope or Gospel? The Crisis of Faith in the Protestant Churches* (Marshall Morgan & Scott, 1982), p.146.
11. Rahner, op. cit., p.300.
12. Quoted in Samuel, op. cit., p.147.
13. Rahner, op. cit., p.286.
14. Ibid., p.300.
15. Ibid.
16. Ibid., pp.296-7.
17. Ibid., p.288.
18. Ibid.
19. Ibid.
20. Ibid., p.289.
21. Ibid., p.347.
22. Ibid., p.348.
23. Ibid., p.349.
24. Ibid., p.296.
25. Ibid., p.260.
26. Ibid., p.261.
27. Ibid., p.300.
28. Ibid., p.295.
29. G.C. Berkouwer, *The Sacraments*, Studies in Dogmatics (Eerdmans, 1969), p.262.
30. See 2 (above). The statement on the eucharist is found on pp.12-25 of *The Final Report*.
31. *The Final Report*, p.3.
32. Ibid., p.2.
33. Ibid., p.11.
34. Ibid., p.17.
35. Ibid., pp.1-2,5.
36. Ibid., p.5.
37. *The Book of Common Prayer* (Oxford University Press, n.d.), pp.686-90.

38. *The Final Report*, p.13.
39. Ibid., p.14.
40. Ibid., p.15.
41. Ibid., p.14 (footnote).
42. Ibid., p.21.
43. Ibid., p.15.
44. Ibid., pp.15-16.
45. Ibid., p.35.
46. Ibid., pp.13-14.
47. Ibid., p.14.
48. Ibid.
49. Ibid., p.12.
50. See list in A.M. Stibbs, *The Finished Work of Christ* (Tyndale Press, 1952), pp.5-7.
51. *The Final Report*, p.20.
52. Quoted in W.H. Griffith Thomas, *The Principles of Theology* (Longmans, Green, 1930), p.423.
53. Quoted in A.M. Stibbs, *Sacrament, Sacrifice and Eucharist* (Tyndale Press, 1961), p.12.
54. *Eucharistic Sacrifice*, edited by J.I. Packer (Church Book Room Press, 1962), p.3.
55. Ibid.
56. Ibid., p.4.
57. Stibbs, *The Finished Work of Christ*, op. cit., pp.5-7.
58. Quoted in Stibbs, *Eucharistic Sacrifice*, p.22.
59. *The Final Report*, p.13.
60. C.F.D. Moule, *The Sacrifice of Christ* (Hodder and Stoughton, 1957), p.67.
61. *Journal of Theological Studies*, new series, 6:2 (October 1955), pp.183f.
62. Packer, op. cit., p.14.
63. John Calvin, *Institutes of the Christian Religion*, Vol. 2 (James Clarke, 1962), p.611 (Book IV, xviii, 5).

Chapter 3. Justification by Faith Alone

1. These articles were published in 1987, but we have been unable to trace the exact date of publication. *Salvation and the Church* itself was published in January of that year.
2. Anglican-Roman Catholic International Commission, *Salvation and the Church* (Church House Publishing/Catholic Truth Society, 1987), pp.6-7.
3. Alister McGrath, 'Justification — "Making Just" or "Declaring Just"?', *Churchman*, 96:1 (1982), pp.50-1.
4. Alister McGrath, *ARCIC II and Justification: an Evangelical Anglican Assessment of 'Salvation and the Church'*, Latimer Studies, no. 26 (Latimer House, 1987), p.4.
5. *Salvation and the Church*, p.7.
6. Ibid., p.6.
7. Ibid., p.26.

8. *'Righteousness' in the New Testament: 'Justification' in the United States Lutheran-Catholic Dialogue*, edited by John Reumann (Fortress/Paulist Press, 1982).
9. See chapter 1, p.12f.
10. McGrath, *ARCIC II and Justification*, p.21.
11. Ibid., p.44.
12. 'A symposium on ARCIC II', *Evangel*, 5:2 (Summer 1987), p.10.
13. Ibid., p.13.
14. McGrath, *ARCIC II and Justification*, pp.26-7.
15. Ibid.
16. *Evangel*, pp.21-4.
17. See chapter 1.
18. *Salvation and the Church*, p.16 (para. 13).
19. Ibid., p.19.
20. McGrath, *ARCIC II and Justification*, p.43.
21. Ibid.
22. See chapter 1.
23. *Salvation and the Church*, p.17.
24. *Evangel*, p.13.
25. See Ronald Y.K. Fung, 'The Forensic Character of Justification', *Themelios*, 3:1 (September 1977), p.19.
26. *Salvation and the Church*, p.14.
27. Ibid., p.15.
28. Ibid., p.20.
29. Ibid., p.19.
30. Ibid.
31. Ibid., p.21.
32. Ibid., p.20. The original quotation comes from Augustine's *Sermons*, 169:13.
33. Ibid., p.16.
34. McGrath, *ARCIC II and Justification*, p.21.
35. *Salvation and the Church*, p.18.
36. McGrath, *ARCIC II and Justification*, pp.26-7.
37. Ibid., p.28.
38. J.I. Packer, 'Introductory Essay' in James Buchanan, *The Doctrine of Justification* (Banner of Truth, 1961), p.7.
39. *Evangel*, p.7.
40. Alister McGrath, 'The Article by which the Church Stands or Falls', *Evangelical Quarterly*, 58:3 (July 1986), p.207. McGrath quotes from the original Latin. The English translation is mine.
41. *Salvation and the Church*, p.19.
42. See Ronald Y.K. Fung, 'The Status of Justification by Faith in Paul's Thought: a Brief Survey of a Modern Debate', *Themelios*, 6:3 (April 1981).
43. *Salvation and the Church*, p.16.
44. McGrath, 'Justification — "Making Just" or "Declaring Just"?', p.49.
45. *Salvation and the Church*, p.17.
46. Ibid.
47. See 'Definitive Sanctification' in John Murray, *Collected Writings of John Murray*, Vol. 2 (Banner of Truth, 1977), pp.277-84.
48. *Evangel*, p.24.

49. *Salvation and the Church*, p.17.
50. J.H. Newman, *Lectures on Justification*, third edition (Longmans, Green, 1874), pp.87ff and 109ff. For an appraisal of this work see Alister McGrath, 'The High Church Misrepresentation of Luther', *Churchman*, 97:2 (1983).
51. 'The Unjustified Case for Church Unity', *The Times* (7 March 1987).
52. *Salvation and the Church*, pp.18-19.
53. McGrath, *ARCIC II and Justification*, p.34.
54. Ibid.
55. Ibid., p.35.
56. *Salvation and the Church*, p.16. See also the next chapter.
57. 'Faith, Hope and a Fresh Wind', *The Times* (21 March 1987).
58. *Church Times*. Exact date unknown.
59. *The Times*. Date unknown.
60. Packer. op. cit., pp.2-3.

Chapter 4. Baptism, Eucharist and Ministry

1. *Baptism, Eucharist and Ministry,* Faith and Order Paper, no. 111 (World Council of Churches, 1982).
2. In a version of the above published by the British Council of Churches, p.2.
3. *Baptism, Eucharist and Ministry*, p.x.
4. *Ecumenical Perspectives on Baptism, Eucharist and Ministry: Theological Essays*, edited by Max Thurian, Faith and Order Paper, no.116 (WCC, 1983), p.viii.
5. Ibid., pp.viii-ix.
6. *Baptism, Eucharist and Ministry*, p.ix.
7. Quoted by David F. Wright in *Baptism, Eucharist & Ministry: (the 'Lima Report'), an Evangelical Assessment*, Rutherford Forum Paper, 3 (Rutherford House, 1984). The quotation comes from *Lima 1982: a Report* (Church of Scotland Inter-Church Relations Committee, 1982).
8. Wright, op. cit., p.2.
9. Ibid., p.2.
10. Ibid.
11. Thurian, op. cit., p.xi.
12. Ibid., p.xi.
13. Ibid., p.xii.
14. Ibid.
15. Ibid., p.5.
16. Ibid. *Lex orandi lex credendi* is a Latin expression which means: 'The rule of praying [is] the rule of believing.'
17. *Baptism, Eucharist and Ministry*, p.ix.
18. Roger Beckwith, 'The Ecumenical Quest for Agreement in Faith', *Themelios*, 10:1 (September, 1984), p.30.
19. Ibid. See Faith and Order Paper no. 59 for the evidence.
20. Beckwith, op. cit., p.29.
21. *Anglican-Orthodox Dialogue: the Moscow Agreed Statement*, edited by Kallistos Ware and Cyril J. Davey (SPCK, 1977).
22. *Baptism, Eucharist and Ministry*, p.11.

23. Beckwith, op. cit., p.29.
24. Gerald L. Bray, *Sacraments and Ministry in Ecumenical Perspective*, Latimer Studies, 18 (Latimer House, 1984), p.9.
25. Ibid., p.5.
26. *Baptism, Eucharist and Ministry*, p.14.
27. Ibid., p.10.
28. Bray, op. cit., p.5.
29. Wright, op. cit., p.8.
30. *Baptism, Eucharist and Ministry*, p.11.
31. Wright, op. cit., p.9.
32. Beckwith, op. cit., p.30.
33. Ibid.
34. See commentary paragraphs 13-15 in *Baptism, Eucharist and Ministry*, pp.12-13.
35. *Baptism, Eucharist and Ministry*, p.13.
36. Ibid.
37. Ibid.
38. Ibid.
39. Ibid.
40. Timothy Ware, *The Orthodox Church* (Penguin, 1976), pp.289-90.
41. Wright, op. cit., p.10.
42. *Baptism, Eucharist and Ministry*, p.12.
43. Ibid., p.4.
44. Ibid., pp.2,3.
45. Ibid., pp.4,6.
46. Wright, op.cit., p.5.
47. Ibid.
48. Ibid.
49. *Baptism, Eucharist and Ministry*, p.3.
50. Ibid., p.2.
51. Ibid.
52. Ibid., p.12.
53. Wright, op.cit., p.12.
54. Ibid., p.6.
55. Herman N. Ridderbos, *Paul: an Outline of his Theology* (SPCK, 1977), p.409.
56. Ibid.
57. Ibid.
58. Ibid., pp.409-10.
59. Ibid., p.410.
60. William Cunningham, *The Reformers and the Theology of the Reformation* (Banner of Truth, 1967), p.240.
61. Wright, op. cit., p.14.
62. *Baptism, Eucharist and Ministry*, p.23.
63. Ibid.
64. Ibid., p.25.
65. Ibid.
66. Ibid., pp.26-7.
67. Ibid., p.29.
68. Ibid.

166

69. Ibid.
70. Wright, op.cit., p.15.
71. *Baptism, Eucharist and Ministry*, p.32.
72. Ibid., p.27.
73. Ibid., p.22.

Chapter 5. Mission and Evangelism

1. *Baptism, Eucharist and Ministry*, Faith and Order Paper, no.111 (World Council of Churches, 1982), pp.viii-ix.
2. H. P. Van Dusen, *One Great Ground of Hope* (Westminster Press, 1961), p.16.
3. Harvey T. Hoekstra, *Evangelism in Eclipse: World Mission and the World Council of Churches* (Paternoster Press, 1979).
4. *Mission and Evangelism: an Ecumenical Affirmation* (World Council of Churches, 1985). At the time of going to press, this work was out of print. The text of *Mission and Evangelism* has, however, been reproduced with its original paragraphs in a British Council of Churches publication (see 23 below). The page numbers given below for quotations from *Mission and Evangelism* refer to this latter work.
5. Ibid., p.vi.
6. Hoekstra, op. cit., p.27.
7. Lesslie Newbiggin, 'Mission and Missions', *Christianity Today* (1 August 1960), p.23. Quoted by Hoekstra, op. cit., pp.27-8.
8. Peter Wagner, *Frontiers in Missionary Strategy*, (Moody Press, 1971), p.54.
9. Hoekstra, op. cit., p.68.
10. Ibid., p.35.
11. *Witness in Six Continents, Mexico City, CWME 1963*, edited by Ronald K. Orchard (Edinburgh House Press, 1964), p.157. Quoted by Hoekstra, op. cit., p.56.
12. Hoekstra, op. cit., p.69.
13. *Uppsala Speaks: the Reports from Uppsala* (World Council of Churches, 1968), p.318.
14. The author has been unable to trace the exact source of this quotation.
15. 'The Frankfurt Declaration on the Fundamental Crisis in Christian Mission', in *One World, One Task: Report of the Evangelical Alliance Commission on World Mission* (Scripture Union, 1971), p.162.
16. Ibid., p.163.
17. Ibid.
18. Ibid., p.164.
19. Ibid., pp.164-5.
20. Ibid., p.165.
21. Ibid., pp.165-6.
22. Hoekstra, op. cit., pp.73-4.
23. John Matthews, *Mission and Evangelism: a Programme for Local Churches* (British Council of Churches, 1984), p.6.

24. R.T. France, 'The Church and the Kingdom of God: Some Hermeneutical Issues', in *Biblical Interpretation and the Church: Text and Context*, edited by D.A. Carson (Paternoster, 1984), p.30.
25. Matthews, op. cit., p.1.
26. Ibid., p.8.
27. Ibid., p.24.
28. See *An International Symposium on the Lausanne Covenant*. See also: *The New Face of Evangelicalism*, edited by René Padilla (Hodder, 1976). J.A. Kirk, *A New World Coming* (Marshall, Morgan & Scott, 1983). Klaus Bockmuehl, *Evangelicals and Social Ethics*, Outreach and Identity: Evangelical Theological Monographs, no.4 (Paternoster, 1979). *Evangelism and Social Responsibility* (Paternoster, 1982).
29. Matthews, op. cit., pp.2,10.
30. Ibid., p.8.
31. Ibid.
32. Ibid.
33. Ibid.
34. Ibid.
35. Ibid., p.10.
36. Ibid.
37. Ibid., p.12.
38. Ibid.
39. Ibid., p.32.
40. R. Runcie, 'Christianity and World Religions', *World Faiths Insight*, new series 14 (October 1986), p.3. This was the Sir Francis Younghusband Memorial Lecture and was delivered on May 28, 1986. Sir Francis was the founder of the World Congress of Faiths.
41. Ibid., p.10.
42. Ibid., p.8.
43. Matthews, op. cit., p.32.
44. Ibid.
45. Translation from German of part of the text of a paper given at a private conference by one who was present at Nairobi.
46. S.J. Samartha, *Courage for Dialogue: Ecumenical Issues in Inter-religious Relationships* (World Council of Churches, 1981), p.62.
47. Ibid.
48. *Gathered for Life: Official Report of the Sixth Assembly*, edited by D. Gill (World Council of Churches, 1983).
49. W.A. Visser 't Hooft, *No Other Name: the Choice between Syncretism and Christian Universalism* (Westminster Press, 1963), p.11.

Postscript

NOTES

NOTES

NOTES

CHRISTIAN HYMNS

First published in 1977, and edited by Paul E.G. Cook and Graham Harrison, *Christian Hymns* is a hymn-book that has received much acclaim for its loyalty to the great truths of the gospel. Its 901 hymns provide a comprehensive selection, with hymns highlighting both the objective and subjective aspects of the Christian life. The inclusion of 80 metrical psalms and paraphrases together with a useful children's section has also been a factor in its wide appeal.

The *music* book has a fine selection of 700 tunes carefully set to appropriate hymns, and for a number of hymns alternative tunes have been suggested. The book also incorporates a larger-than-usual selection of Welsh tunes, and a number of translations of Welsh hymns, some of them specially written for *Christian Hymns*.

Some press comments:

'Superb . . . the finest available.' — *Focus*

'Here is the beating heart of evangelical hymnody.' — *Crusade*

'A fine piece of work . . . accompanied by pastoral insights into the needs of the average congregation.' — *Banner of Truth*

'A fine hymn-book . . . a monumental task superbly performed.' — *Fellowship*

'Cannot be bettered.' — *Symphony*

'Congregational hymn-singing will be much improved through the regular use of this collection of hymns.' — *Evangelical Times*

From letters received:

'The new hymn-book has been a tremendous blessing to us.'

'A great help in the worship and experience of the church.'

'It restores an element of assurance and joy lacking from some compilations.'

'It will be recommended by us as often as possible.'

'Has enriched us as a church and also as a family.'

'The best thing to happen to hymn-singing this century!'

REVIVAL

CHRISTIAN HANDBOOK

by

Peter Jeffery

This new handbook provides a basic introduction to the Bible, church history and Christian doctrine. In *one* handy volume it therefore provides a range of information which would otherwise only be found either in much larger and more expensive publications, or in a large number of smaller ones. Written in a plain and straightforward style, it will prove invaluable not only for the new Christian but for all who want to broaden their knowledge of the Christian faith.

- Over 90 illustrations including maps, charts, drawings and photographs.
- A comprehensive index.
- Available in hardback and paperback.

'This is a great little handbook, the best of its kind. Let every church buy a copy for each new convert; it's just what they need.' — Brian H. Edwards in *Evangelicals Now*

'This book is packed with information that every Christian needs to know. It is an ideal handbook for young people, Christians and all who wish to broaden their knowledge of the Christian faith.' — David Barker in *Grace*

Other titles by Peter Jeffery published by the Evangelical Press of Wales

Seeking God

A clear explanation of the gospel for those who are really looking for salvation in Christ.

All Things New

A simple, down-to-earth explanation of what it means to be a Christian and to live the Christian life.

Walk Worthy

Clear guidelines about prayer, the Bible, the local church, evangelism, assurance, work, marriage, money and other issues that every Christian has to face.

Stand Firm

A young Christian's guide to the armour of God.

Our Present Sufferings

An excellent little book to put in the hands of those who are going through a period of suffering.

Firm Foundations (with Owen Milton)

An introduction to the great chapters of the Bible. This book takes the form of a two-month course of daily Bible readings together with a helpful commentary on each passage.

Books on contemporary issues published by Evangelical Press of Wales:

SOCIAL ISSUES AND THE LOCAL CHURCH

Ian Shaw (editor)

Among the subjects covered by this work are: the Christian and the state, the Christian concern for education, the role of women in the church, social welfare and the local church and mission in today's world.

CHRISTIAN FAMILY MATTERS

Ian Shaw (editor); foreword by Sir Frederick Catherwood

Here is clear biblical teaching by experienced contributors on marriage, parenthood, childhood and adolescence, the handicapped child, fostering and adoption, divorce, abortion and family planning, and the care of the elderly.

THE CHRISTIAN, THE CHURCH AND DAILY WORK

Gerallt Wyn Davies

In this little book the author looks at biblical teaching regarding work, compares it with society's attitudes, and outlines what individual Christians and the church could do to be of effective help in alleviating the great social problem of unemployment.